Why I Am Me

Surviving Grief and Trauma

By Danielle Sternquist

i

Cover Design by: Creation Station Central

Contents

NEW BEGINNINGS 1

MY SECOND YEAR 8

THE FIRST BIG MOVE 14

THE BEST AND WORST OF SUMMERS...................................23

LIFE IN DELANO 30

FIRST GRADE..37

MOVING TO CALIFORNIA..41

LIFE IN CALIFORNIA..46

NEW FAMILY MEMBERS..53

BACK TO MINNESOTA...62

PRINCESS AND BLOSSOM 73

ROUGHING IT 81

DECEPTION 92

FOSTER CARE...103

HAWICK 111

CLEARWATER 123

MARRIED LIFE..132

BABY BRIANNA 137

GRANDPA 144

BACK TO CLEAR LAKE 150

JAYDEN 154

THE ACCIDENT...158

NEW HOUSE-NEW BEGINNINGS 166

MARRIED 171

MY GROWN-UP KIDS 178

2012...186

AFTER JAYDEN'S DEATH 198

NEW FAMILY 205

HEALING..210

THE PERFECT STORM..216

v

DEDICATION

I am dedicating this book to all the people that shaped me. I would not be the person I am today if I had not had the life I have had. Jesus has been watching me all along even if I was not paying attention to him. Just know that Jesus is always by your side and all you must do is accept him.

This is a story of my life as I saw it. I have been told that my story is interesting and I am writing in hopes that I can help someone out there who has had similar things happen to them. My viewpoints are mine alone and others in my story may have different viewpoints on what or how things happened. I have changed the names to protect those that are in my life that I do not want to be hurt. I chose to not have this edited professionally so any mistakes are mine. As you read you will see that I do not follow Jesus at every point in my life but just as the bible says, train up a child in the way they should go and when he is old, he will not depart from it; Proverbs 22:6. I think this describes me because Jesus has called me to come back several times in my life and in the end He is my Lord and Savior and I am A child of God.

NEW BEGINNINGS

The Sixties were a time of change, but also a time of very conservative values. In Minnesota in 1963 very few people had a child out of wedlock; if they did it was generally frowned upon and covered up with a very quick wedding or they were sent away to a home for unwed mothers, or sent away for an abortion. My mother grew up in this time trying like most of us to fit in a society where we do not feel like we fit in. My grandparents raised my mother in a small town in Minnesota. Delano is a very small town in central Minnesota and the people there are conservative and for the most part, Catholic. My family was not Catholic and my grandma was raised up in a conservative church, her parents being very devout. My grandparents liked to go out bowling with friends or go play cards at each other's houses. At the time they both drank but my grandma quit drinking and went back to the church eventually. When my mom graduated, she went to live with her grandparents in Guthrie Center, Iowa; where they ran the Town Club. She turned eighteen that fall and she was having a great time being single. She was working for her grandparents, this offered her a great way to save money. She had plans to attend the University of Minnesota Veterinary Program. Unfortunately, or fortunately depending on how you look at it, sometime in October 1963 she met up with a man I know nothing about. My mother became pregnant with this man's child, but the circumstances were never explained to me. It is crazy to not ever know where you came from or who you came from for that matter. This is a part of my life that I knew nothing about until I was 16. I know there are many people out there who have the same or similar circumstances, but for me it has always left a giant hole in a place that should be filled. My grandpa always tried to fill that role.

Sometimes I look at my life and wonder if I would be considered a mistake. Is anyone a mistake in the eyes of God? There was always abortion or adoption in those days, but my mom chose none of these. She chose to go back home at Christmas time and explain to her family that she was going to have a baby, sometime in July 1964. My oldest Uncle was thrilled to have A new niece or nephew but my grandparents shushed him and told him he is not to talk about it. If this had been 2008 instead of 1963 things would be vastly different, largely because God has been taken out of families and government. My biological father was not going to be in the picture and my mother was not given the option of telling him about the pregnancy. Mainly because she did not know how to get ahold of him. She was brave and gave up a lot to be able to bring me into this world and for that I am grateful because God has a plan for every baby. My Mom moved to Minneapolis where she could get a job to support us. I recall her telling me that she lived in an apartment and shared it with a roommate. She waitressed so and saved money for the two of us. I was born in Minneapolis on July 26th 1964 and weighed 6lbs 4oz.and was

21 inches long. Mom said I was very long and skinny and that I looked like a plucked chicken! Babies never seem to be born looking like the Gerber Baby so I guess it is no surprise that I did not look like one either. One thing is certain, God does not make mistakes. He knew me before I was even conceived and he knows how it will end.

By September of 1964 we had moved back to Delano and Mom continued to work as a waitress. My great grandmother was taking care of me. During that first winter of 1964-1965 we did not have a phone, you can imagine what that would be like with a little baby. My grandparents were building a house on 13 acres they bought. The Crow River ran past the house and land which was lowland, and just outside of Delano. They were living in the basement of the house that they were working on. I can imagine this was a tight squeeze with myself and my mother added in. The winter was a bad one. We do not seem to have winters like that anymore, with more snow than can be shoveled and bitter cold. Unbeknownst to us mother nature was not through with us yet. My grandparents decided to take a trip to their cabin they had bought in McGregor, Minnesota. They left on St. Patrick's Day from the river house (that is what we always called it) with the intention of coming home that Sunday. Forecasts in those days were not as reliable as they are today. Little did they know that a snowstorm was about to hit that would snow them in for days and make living at the river house almost impossible either to live in or get out of, and to top it off I was very sick. During this time my great grandparents (whom I lovingly called grandma and grandpa at the club) were staying out at the house with us and helping us through the storm. My uncles were only 9 and 10 years older than I was, so my great grandparents were watching them while my grandparents were at the cabin. over them. Thank goodness grandpa at the club was there because being stranded is hard enough, but being stranded with an eight-month-old baby who happens to be very sick is even worse. I cannot imagine the worry my mother went through with an infant that is running a very high fever and the feeling of being totally closed in with no way out to the road. I bet many prayers were said during this time for a sick baby and better weather that was making things impossible. This was the first of many bouts of illness for me in my life. Mom did not know at the time, but I was very sick with pneumonia. She decided that I needed to get to the doctor as soon as possible but with a four-foot drift of snow in the driveway it was nearly impossible to even think about going anywhere, let alone with a sick baby. With no phone and no way out of the driveway by vehicle, my mom had to get bundled up and trudge that half - mile long driveway to the neighbor's house to use the phone. The house was set way back in the woods with a view of the river. In the summer the driveway was great, it allowed privacy, but in the winter, it was a different story! She made a call to the township snow plow crew and they were able to come to our rescue and plow the driveway so we could get out to the doctor. My mom and grandpa at the club drove me to Watertown to the nearest doctor. It did not take the doctor long to discover that I had pneumonia and prescribed antibiotics. Penicillin was the usual course of antibiotics at the time. By the time we got home, the driveway was once again impassable and the township crew had to come and open it back up for us to get back home where it was warm and cozy. Unfortunately, this was not the last of the problems because of this massive blizzard; everyone woke up

Saturday morning to find that the fuel oil had run out and the house was very cold. With a sick baby and two young boys we could not be without heat. My grandpa at the club and my uncle Dan trudged with toboggans and empty fuel cans back out the half-mile long driveway, where a passing farmer gave them a ride to town to get fuel. This farmer was kind enough to wait and give them a ride back to the end of the driveway as well. That winter we had a near record 93 inches of snow, which would lead to a very interesting spring.

MY SECOND YEAR

Everyone was glad when it seemed that spring was right around the corner and we would get a reprieve from the weather for a while, but little did we know that this was only the beginning. My grandparents house they were building was located on the Crow River. You could not ask for a more beautiful setting for this house, it was my grandparents dream home. They had built another house previously in Delano so they were no stranger to hard work and living without certain amenities. The river House as we all called it was my first real home and I loved this house and the feeling of security it brought me. I considered this my home and loved to be there with all my family. The spring of 1965 seemed to come all at once and the melting of the snow was a happy sight, that is until you realize how much snow we have and how fast it is melting. When snow is that deep and melts that fast, the river is sure to flood its banks and that is just what it did. There were a lot of people in Delano that had to evacuate due to the tremendous amount of water that inhabited Delano. My grandparents, along with my mom and Uncles were fighting tooth and nail to keep the water out of the house. They had to haul furniture, clothing, and dishes to the upstairs and tear off the paneling in the basement to prevent further damage. The water just kept rising and would leave a watermark on the walls in the basement to remind us how high the water progressed that spring. It did not take long to see that the basement was completely flooded by the water from dirt and silt that was the Crow River. This included many inhabitants of the Crow River; snakes and frogs just to mention a few. No amount of sandbagging could stop this mighty Crow from overflowing its banks. We moved to town to stay with my great grandparents, while overhead helicopters with news crews flew and recorded the rising water in the town of Delano. The desperation and sadness on the faces of the towns' people can be seen in the home movies and old newsreels. Rivers are not supposed to flow down the main streets of town. Unfortunately staying with my great grandparents did not last long and we had to evacuate once again. My great grandparents went to my great aunts in St. Louis Park and my grandparents stayed with friends in town up on Third Street in Delano, where the water had not yet reached. The flood stage for the Crow River was 8 feet and when it rose that spring it crested at 18.4 feet. This flood has not been rivaled in forty plus years! Times were different back then; there was not any help from the government. Nobody came knocking on the door with food, money, or clothes. Nobody had benefits or fundraisers for help and there also was not any Go Fund Me. People had hard times and they struggled through hard times, they knew how to make ends meet and how to overcome adversity due to growing up in the depression era and post-World War II. My Mom and Grandmother spent days and weeks cleaning up the mess that the flood left behind. In my grandmother's book, Hardships & Joys which was never published except for family, she states the high-water mark in the basement was over six feet. Because of the mess and the fact that the basement was still damp from the flood mom and

I stayed at my great grandparents. After the flood went down my great grandma at the club babysat me at the house in town.

We resided in a small trailer house behind my grandparent's house for a time. I was told one time of being in my crib one sunny day that summer and my grandpa found some tiny wild rabbits and placed them in my crib so I could see them. I have been told that I would spend an endless amount of time with my grandparents. My grandma would pack up a picnic lunch and we would go out into the woods and watch the wildlife and have a picnic. If mom happened to be cooking something I did not like, I would toddle over to my grandparents to see what grandma was cooking. It was then that I would decide who had the better meal and where I would eat. Mind you I was two years old at the time. This is the earliest memory I have of the river house. This was an idyllic time for my family and me. Pictures and movies show the innocence of the times. My family was very much into music; my grandma and my mom played and sang, my mom played guitar and my grandma played the piano. While still in diapers I danced to the music with my uncles, Dan, and Jon, with my grandpa looking on. Cousins from the cities would come out on the weekends, and along with my grandma's brother, they would play wonderful gospel and country western music. My Mom was an awesome singer, I think she missed her calling! My Mom started dating Jake who later adopted me, unbeknownst to me, and became my dad. They were married in September 1966. I was about two and a half at the time.

My mother was always protective of me and through her I was told of a time we went to my grandma and grandpa Schticks house in Mound, Minnesota for Thanksgiving. My dad's family was very dysfunctional and several of them were alcoholics, including my grandparents. When we got to their house nobody was home and we waited until my dad finally had to get them out of the bar, this of course was completely the opposite of my maternal grandparents and the family time we spent with them. The turkey had not even been started and I was very hungry. My mom got me a hamburger, packed me up and told my dad we were leaving and would never again come to their house for Thanksgiving. I do not ever remember visiting them again. We always celebrated Thanksgiving with my grandma and grandpa in Delano Minnesota.

THE FIRST BIG MOVE

During 1967 when I was three years old my mom, dad and I moved to Charlotte, South Carolina, after my dad re-enlisted in the navy. This was a very hard move for me; I had been virtually living with my grandparents, the security I felt with them at the river House was never again rivaled. Their separation from me was equally, if not harder on my grandparents since I was their first and only grandchild. Mom and dad bought a house in Charlotte, South Carolina. It was cozy and quaint. It was brick with hardwood floors and throw rugs to complement. There was a fenced in back yard where I could have a dog, so we got Sailor, a white German shepherd and a little gray kitty. My mother was not used to being away from the family in Minnesota. She soon found out that she was going to be having a baby and being pregnant made the times that much harder for her.

The Vietnam war was going full force. My dad was deployed to Vietnam in 1968 and while the unrest was going on overseas there was another kind going on here at home. My mother was pregnant with my little brother and with the baby coming and her all alone with a toddler, it would soon become apparent that it would be too hard for her to be all alone with me as she drew nearer to delivery. She came to the decision that it would be better for me to go visit my grandparents until she was settled in with the new baby. My grandpa flew to Charlotte South Carolina to pick me up and we flew back to Delano on March 23, 1968. Upon arrival to Delano, my grandmother's niece was getting married. Sara and Ron had a beautiful wedding and since it was the first wedding I had been to it was even more special to me. When I got to grandmas we had to drive to Minneapolis where the wedding was to take place, but the travel on the plane was wearing on me and according to grandma, I managed to stay awake for the processional down the aisle. I proceeded to exclaim "isn't her beautiful," and I fell sound asleep on my grandma's lap. According to my grandma's book, she saved me a piece of wedding cake and was glad she did because I was looking for it the next morning when I woke up. My young life was just getting started and while I stayed with grandma and

Grandpa, I was about to turn four, I began Sunday school at the Evangelical Free Church in Delano and met a couple of good friends. I loved Sunday school and especially singing the songs we sang. When I listen to them now it brings back memories of my Sunday school days. They were the best days.

The world continued to be violent; with the war in Vietnam, people were very disrespectful to the men that came back from the war. They would protest, hold sit ins and at times when the men came home in their uniforms instead of welcoming them home, people would throw eggs and garbage at them. Many enlisted men chose to come home in their street clothes to avoid the confrontations at the airport. I have a difficult time imagining what those poor soldiers went through because a generation later they are honored and made heroes for their efforts in defending our freedoms. The month after I returned to Delano, Martin Luther King was assassinated, of course being in central Minnesota this did not affect us as much as it did elsewhere. I never really understood what went on with Dr. King until I studied about him in college. Up until this point, I do not believe I had ever even seen a person of color anywhere around me. I could not appreciate the fact that I had been born into a white middle-class family.

My brother was born on May 8, 1968. Finally, I was a big sister! It was not long after that my mom came and got me from my grandparents in Minnesota and flew us all back to North Carolina. Soon after that my grandparents came to visit. My grandma never missed a birthday, until I was in my 30's. They flew all the way to Charlotte, to spend my 4th birthday with me. I was very excited and recall how surprised I was to see them. Apparently, they missed me so much they could not stand to stay away. I was so sad that they could only stay a week and when they went to leave, I laid down in the driveway behind their car in hopes that it would convince them to stay. I loved my grandma and grandpa.

I recall while we were in Charlotte, we sometimes had snow in the winter and I was able to go sliding. The snow was very wet and sticky, but that never deterred me from attempting to slide. My mother would cut the bottom off a cardboard box and that is what I would use to slide on. With the small hill in the backyard, I was able to play outside and feel like I was in

Minnesota, of course the snow did not last long in the south. My mother was always a stay-at-home mom; she did not have a career and spent her time raising us. My puppy Sailor was a great companion; he was sweet and was a great friend and I played with him a lot. One afternoon a boy from the subdivision came over and he was being cruel to Sailor, he twisted his tail and tried to tie a knot in it and Sailor proceeded to bite him. My mom always had a rule if a dog bites, he does not get another chance, even if it was not his fault. I was told that we had to take Sailor to the pound because he had bitten this boy. I recall taking him to the pound and crying because it was not his fault. I also had a great little kitty that I loved so much; I was a true animal lover and of course kitties being kitties, one winter morning my mother had to wake me to tell me that my kitty had crawled up into the warm engine of our car and when dad started it kitty was killed. What a sad day that was for a little girl of four; I recall sitting on the edge of my bed with my mothers' arms around me while tears streamed down my face. As a mother she of course tried to comfort me and probably felt worse than I did. I always felt so secure with my mother.

During our stay in Charlotte, my mother tried to get me to go to preschool, but there was no way I was getting on that bus and leaving my mom, so after trudging up the hill to take me to the bus and me crying and refusing to get on, my mom had to apologize to the bus driver and trudge back down the hill with me in tow. I guess I was just not ready to leave her side yet.

I was always so proud that my dad was in the Navy; I even had a little white sailor outfit that I wore when I was four. Then I could be just like my dad! One of the downfalls to being in the Navy is that they get shipped out an awful lot. With the Vietnam war still raging, my dad was once again shipped to Vietnam. I did not know it at the time, but my dad was an alcoholic and he proceeded to get thrown in the brig for drinking while on duty. The Navy gave him a choice of getting out of the Navy or going to Vietnam on another tour and he chose the tour. My mother was very angry and rightly so. She was pregnant with my sister and she decided that this tour would be a long one, so we decided to move back in with my grandparents in Delano. The basement of the river house was not being used now, so it would be a perfect solution for us all. My mom thought that it might be easier to send me on an airplane to my grandma and grandpa's instead of traveling by car with a youngster and a baby. So, the plan was set, they tried to get a flight close to home, but it would mean that I would have to transfer flights and with me only being four years old, that was not an option. So, instead they booked me a flight out of Atlanta, Georgia. We traveled there from our house in Charlotte. To make it more fun for me, my mom and dad took us to Six Flags Over Georgia, a theme park in Atlanta. We stayed overnight in a hotel and went to the airport the next day. We arrived at the airport in plenty of time, if you were going to the Minneapolis-St. Paul airport, but the Atlanta airport had a huge concourse. My mom and dad started walking with me in tow and by the time they got to the gate they were at a dead run with my little brother and a four-year old which I imagine it was quite a sight. When they got me to the gate the airplane was waiting for me and my mom had barely enough time to say goodbye. With tears streaming down my face, I told her I changed my mind and did not want to go, I just wanted to stay with my mom. I was lovingly told that my kitty was already on the plane and so were my clothes, and that grandma and grandpa were waiting for me in Minnesota, so still not totally convinced, I stood at the doorway of the plane in my beautiful yellow dress and matching coat and waved. My mother waved goodbye, blew me kisses and sent me on my way. The pilots were waiting just for me knowing that grandma and grandpa would be at the airport in Minneapolis Minnesota. I was like most children as soon as I got on the airplane and buckled up with my own stewardess. She got me a glass of seven up, which I promptly spilled all over my beautiful dress. I was upset about my dress and worried about leaving my mom but in the end, everything turned out fine.

Just like my mom said, my grandma and grandpa were waiting at the gate. The stewardess had specific instructions to ask my grandparents for ID, but when I got off the plane and saw my grandpa no ID was necessary. I ran as hard as my little legs could carry me and jumped into the waiting arms of my grandpa. My mom and dad came shortly thereafter because they drove home to Minnesota with our belongings. During the summer that I was four, I found my love of horses. My grandfather had cows in the pasture, which of course I liked, but that summer he came home with two beautiful quarter horses, Buck and Cricket. Buck was a quarter horse gelding and was a beautiful buckskin color and Cricket was a palomino mare. Grandpa would lead me around on Buck in the front yard and I was never afraid, even though they were big horses. When Cricket was purchased, she was in foal. Nobody knew this until one winter night when the temperatures dipped well below zero and cricket went into labor. She delivered a palomino foal that was premature. The foal did not survive. Everyone believed that the cold weather we had was the reason for her early delivery.

THE BEST AND WORST OF SUMMERS

We spent the next year and a half with my grandparents while my dad was once again shipped to Vietnam. Little did I know that my dad was getting shipped over to Vietnam because his drinking had once again become an issue. This was just one of many lies my father had told my mother including borrowing money from my grandparents and lying to my mom to cover up his drinking. Of course, at the time I had no knowledge of this because my mom protected us from this kind of behavior in our lives. I never knew my father had a drinking problem until many years later as a pre-teen. He came to pick us up, at the farm for visitation, and there was a bottle of Schnapps in the back seat on the floor of his car.

The summer of my sixth birthday started out wonderful, while staying at the river house with my grandma and grandpa. My grandma and grandpa had a wonderful dog. His name was Puppy. He was a probably a cross between a lab and a golden retriever. He had a 'golden' personality. This dog watched over me as a child and he was my best friend. If I wandered anywhere near the river he would stand in my way and not allow me to go near it. I played with Puppy and he kept me safe. He was a good boy and I loved him. We would laugh at him because he never had much energy and would not even chase the rabbits in the yard. One time we looked outside on the patio and a skunk was eating Puppy's dog food, we thought that it either had rabies or it was somebody's pet. Puppy of course just let him eat. We called Puppy in and my grandpa got his gun out to shoot the skunk. The skunk went around the outside of the house back towards my grandma's bedroom. It was not long and we heard a shot and then we smelled him, and did he stink. My grandma was getting ready to go to church to sing in the choir and little did she know that she too smelled like a skunk. When she got to church everyone was saying; "does anyone smell skunk?" The smell in the house lingered for days, but we did not have to worry about a rabid skunk any more thanks to my grandpa. In the winter little chick-a-dee's would come and eat on the patio as well. They were fat little birds that were as round as they could be with little black wings and a little black cap; they looked like fat little round men with a little hat. They were so cute and my mom and grandma would sing me the chick-a-dee song. My grandma would insert my name into the song, it goes like this:

Lisa looked out of the window to see

A poor little bird singing chick a dee dee

Oh, he's so cold can't you see

Yet he keeps singing his chick a dee dee

Chick a dee dee, Chick a dee dee

He's all the time singing his Chick a dee dee

Mama, won't you buy him some shoes

A nice little coat and a hat if you choose

For he's so cold can't you see

Still, he keeps singing Chick a dee dee

We had a huge garden with sweet corn, peas, beans, cucumbers, tomatoes, and several other vegetables, too many to mention, and I got to help in the garden. We could play on the thirteen acres to our hearts content. I was a little tomboy and would catch snakes and frogs and keep them in the stock tank and eventually let them go. We would also catch little baby snapping turtles that were about the size of a silver dollar and have turtle races. There was so much to do at the river house you never ran out of interesting things to explore. The summer wore on and I was fascinated with my uncles. They were nine and ten years older than me and I thought they were wonderful. My uncle Dan was always watching out for me and we were like brother and sister. I would annoy him and he would tell on me. We watched TV together a lot; our favorite shows were Batman, Gilligans Island and the Monkees. I had the habit like most little kids of standing directly in front of the TV when he was watching it. He would get annoyed and holler and then grandma would scold him for hollering at me. Dan was going to become a wonderful artist and I loved seeing what he could draw. I always looked up to him and we had a special bond. We still hold a special bond to this day.

My other uncle Jon was a musician. He was shy and kept to himself. He would always be in his bedroom with the door shut listening to records and playing guitar. I was fascinated with the music and loved to listen to him play and listen to his records. He had many of the old record albums like Cat Stevens, The

Rolling Stones, and Three Dog Night. What I did not know is that he was in some way not normal, he was introverted and did not really have any relationships with girls. In my innocence I trusted him because I never had a reason not to trust anyone. I was only six and had never had anyone hurt me physically or otherwise. I spent a lot of time with him not knowing that I was being manipulated and groomed and that my trust was to be put to the test. This led me to be sexually abused by him over that very summer that I so looked forward to. I was never threatened like you hear on television. He made it seem almost like a game, I was not afraid and went along with what he wanted. Even though I was only six, I had a feeling that the way he touched me and the way he had me touch him was wrong. It was sneaky, under blankets, in the closet. I have flashbacks of being in a closet with bi-fold doors with slats. It is dark in there, but I see the sun on the outside of the door. In here he had me do things that no little girl should have to do, ever. Later, I always felt dirty and ashamed. I was brought up in the church and for a long time I felt responsible for this act. I grew up feeling as though this part of my life was a dream and, in some way, it was my fault. How could someone that I trusted and loved do something like this to me; I cannot recall how many times the molestation abuse occurred but I do know it was several times over the summer. I hope other little girls can see it is not their fault if this happens to them. During my counseling I was taught to imagine that closet and imagine Jesus with me and what he would do. He would put a hand on me and protect me from that abuse. Having this image in my mind has helped me overcome some of the abuse issues.

Because I was so close to my grandma, I told her about the abuse by my uncle. I do not know how I told her but in my little six-year-old mind- I thought I was very clear. Grandma either did not believe me or did not want to believe me because she told me that I must have dreamed it. I think that is where the feeling that I dreamed up the whole thing came from. Finding out later my grandmother had been abused by her brother helped me to understand why she never did anything. As an adult, she told me nobody ever helped her and she turned out just fine. This is how sexual abuse and molestation was handled back then and sometimes still is. There was not anyone that came to our school to explain good touch and bad touch, your mother did not talk to you about it because if you have never been molested you cannot believe that someone you know so well could do that to you. Unfortunately, what occurred that summer has lasted my lifetime and has left scars and implications in its wake. Nobody can go through sexual abuse, especially by someone they trust without being scarred. I learned very early on in my life to equate love with sex and to keep secrets at all costs. Unfortunately, I never told my mother until many years past. When I did tell her it was because my uncle had molested his stepdaughter the same way and by finding this out, I felt that was my fault too, for not telling anyone else in the family. I wonder to this day how many other little girls went through what I did. Not being believed can cause a tremendous amount of trauma.

LIFE IN DELANO

My grandma was very active in our church in Delano, since she taught Sunday school and sang in the choir. I sang my first solo, at the age of 4, in the Delano Free Church. It was "Oh How I Love Jesus" and my grandma accompanied me on the piano. I would go on Saturdays to the church with grandma to clean. She would take a turn with the other ladies to clean the church, during one of these times at about 8 years old I got on my knees and accepted Jesus into my heart. I felt so free and I truly loved Jesus and wanted to be a good girl for Jesus. Me and my grandma also went to the retirement home in Delano to visit the old people there. My grandma would play the piano and we would sing songs like "This Little Light of Mine or Fishers of Men." Songs I learned in Sunday School for the residents uplifted them and gave them a fun afternoon. I really liked going there, it was like having a whole bunch of grandmas and grandpas to see. One lady that I still remember to this day was a very old woman that was very senile. She just sat in her wheel chair and held a doll she had. In her mind she must have been a young woman because she held that doll and talked to it and told everyone it was her baby. She really influenced me because my mom said I talked about her for days after seeing her. It is funny how certain people have a lasting effect on you and you remember them forever. I do not even remember her name, but I do remember how caring she was to her "baby."

Our church in Delano always did many fun things. One of the biggest memories I have about the church is when they had a father-daughter banquet. Of course, my dad was not with us, he was in Vietnam so I did not have a father to go to the banquet with. My grandpa stepped in and went with me. I had a beautiful, new frilly pink dress. I am sure this was difficult for him; if you knew my grandpa you knew he never liked to get dressed up in a suit. My grandpa was a hard worker; he worked as a monument setter for the Delano Granite Works as far back as I can remember. He worked with his hands and it was a hard job as well a dirty one. But when he took me to that banquet, he was all dressed up in a leisure suit (do not laugh) that was the style back then. My grandpa always wore Aqua Velva and if I close my eyes and think back, I can still smell him kind of spicy and clean. I remember by grandpa as a very handsome man. He had pitch-black hair and a ruddy complexion, very much like Johnny Cash. In my mind he was the strongest man I ever knew. I was always very proud of my grandpa. My grandpa was always so caring and he watched out for his family like no one I ever knew. We had a wonderful time at the father-daughter banquet, we ate wonderful food and they had a wishing well that if you put a penny in it, you would get your wish. My grandpa of course gave me a shiny copper penny that I put in the wishing well and I made my wish. My wish, being the horse crazy kid that I was, was for my very own pony. I remember how excited I was after I made that wish. The night could not go fast enough. After all, if you made a wish like that in church it was sure to come true. Because as a little girl, I knew that if you asked Jesus for something he would get it for you. I did not know Jesus did not use wishing wells! Little did I know that Jesus works in his own time and sometimes, if it is not good for you, he will not give you what you want. After the banquet I tore home and ran out to the barn because I just knew there would be a pony waiting for me. I looked in the barn and it was just as empty as when we left. I cannot describe the disappointment I felt; my pony was not there.

My mom and grandparents had a surprise birthday party for me. My birthday was July 26th and my grandpas was July 24th, so many times we spent our birthdays together. This birthday, they invited my friends from the neighborhood and church. I was going to be surprised and we were all going to get to swim in the pool my grandpa had set up. My mom led me down the outside steps to our patio that was under the deck of the river house. The first thing I saw was a big piece of plywood standing on its side. My first reaction was to think; "there must be a pony behind that plywood." I knew that this time my wish was going to come true, after all it was my birthday so what better present to give a little girl than her very own pony. When I got down to the patio all my friends jumped out and said happy birthday. They had whistles and hats and were all excited that we were having a party. Little did they know that I was truly disappointed because there was not a pony behind that piece of plywood. It did not take me long to decide to have a good time anyway and we opened presents and ate cake and then we all went swimming. It was a joyful 6th birthday after all.

My Mom was heavily pregnant with my sister that late summer and my brother was a handful. My mom was due with my sister in approximately two weeks, the weather was hot in August as it usually is and she was canning tomatoes for the winter; canning tomatoes is a hot job and when you are eight and a half months pregnant it is a whole lot of work. My brother was out riding his tricycle on the patio so she continued her canning when she checked again, she saw him heading towards the river. With a look of terror, she dropped everything and ran towards that river and rescued my little brother. The river was not very deep in August, but a toddler can drown in inches of water so for a mother this is a terrifying experience.

A few weeks later my great grandparents were going to have their golden wedding anniversary on August 30th, 1970 at my great aunt's house in Amery, Wisconsin. I really loved my great grandparents; they lived in a log cabin in the woods of Clear Lake, Wisconsin. My great grandfather built this log house as a young man for his bride, and soon to be family. My grandmother was born in this one room cabin in 1925. I remember visiting with them in the log house. Their floor was crooked, it had a hump in the middle of the main room and I recall tripping on that many times. My great grandpa would spin his own wool and knit beautiful mittens. He had a beautiful loom in which he would make rag rugs. Sometimes he would even let me help with the rugs. I would put the shuttle between the warp and then my great grandpa would tamp down the rags and it was not long before we had made a beautiful rag rug. Who would have guessed that you could make something so beautiful out of rags. I wonder if Joseph in the bible's coat of many colors was made from different fabric, like the rugs?

My mom could not go with us to the 50th anniversary because the new baby was due at any moment. My dad stayed home with her and I got to go with grandma and grandpa to the celebration. The next day September 1st, 1970 was another big day. It was the day that I got a baby sister. and soon after my dad was sent to Vietnam. He would be gone close to a year this time. It always seemed like such a long time but to a little girl a year is forever. A year after that special anniversary in August 1971, my great grandma suffered a massive stroke and went into a coma. She died a few hours later. I remember going to that funeral, it must have been the first one I had attended. I can clearly remember her in the casket looking so peaceful. I don't even remember being sad. Maybe I did not know I was supposed to be sad at the time. My great grandpa moved into my great-aunt's house to live. My great grandpa would come sometimes to visit at my grandma's house; he was very frail and had to sit in a wheel chair. He loved the beautiful granite fireplaces in my grandparents' home, and would sit by the fire and enjoy his time visiting with my grandmother. He always saw the best in everything and was very sweet. My great grandpa died at the age of ninety on July 5, 1972.

FIRST GRADE

The winter of 1970-1971 I attended grade school at Delano; my teacher was Mrs. Gillco. One of my earliest memories of first grade was the fact that I was sick a lot. One time I woke up in the morning with a sore throat and the diarrhea, I decided I would need a note for school when I got better, so I wrote my own note. It went like this: "Please excuse Lisa, she has a sore thot and the diary." My grandmother saved that note for all these years and I just recently got it back after she passed away.

I really liked school, although I frequently got in trouble for talking. I was a sweet child, very innocent and I do not believe I had ever been spanked. When I started school and found out that if I got a check after my name for some infraction in class, usually talking, I had to stand on my tiptoes, while Mrs. Gillco wrote a line on the blackboard with chalk. While on my tiptoes, if I dare came down below the line, I would get wacked with a ruler. This was devastating to me, as I stood on my tiptoes with tears streaming down my face, I could imagine the class watching me being spanked. My feelings and my behind were hurt when this would happen. Of course, I do not remember that happening to anyone else even though I am sure it did. This day and age, she probably would go to jail for abuse, but then I guess she thought she was doing right by us. I was a good student even though I was a social butterfly. I loved to learn and still do to this day. Reading was my favorite and I loved the Fun with Dick and Jane books.

Mrs. Gillco knew my love of horses and oh how I wished for a pony. She made a deal with me that if I could go the rest of the school year without a check behind my name, she would give me a pony for the summer. Well, it did not take much convincing, I was anxious to begin. I worked so hard and I would always raise my hand in class to not break the talking rule. It was amazing, I was able to make it the rest of the school year without a check behind my name and Mrs. Gillco lived up to her end of the bargain.

My mother took me out to Mrs. Gillco's farm and dropped me off. Mrs. Gillco said I had to take lessons before I could take the pony home. I would ride and then Mrs. Gillco would make us a lunch. She had goats so we would drink ice-cold goat's milk with our sandwiches. I was so excited I could hardly stand it, my own pony! Who would have thought it could happen to me. Mrs. Gillco saddled up Thunder, he was a beautiful sorrel with a white blaze, he looked like a shiny copper penny and I fell in love at first sight. She took me down to where she would ride and basically turned me loose. Little did she know that I had never ridden a horse on my own; I had only ridden Buck and Cricket the Quarter Horses that my grandpa owned and then only while being led.

I was proud as I rode Thunder around, he pranced and danced and I felt on top of the world, then in the blink of an eye, that little pony took off for the barn. He was living up to his name as he thundered toward the barn and the other horses, of course I had never been on a runaway before and I was terrified. Before I knew it, I was jerked off the saddle by catching my foot on a big wooden post and I hit that post square between the eyes. I bet you never heard such a scream. I sure had a set of lungs on me. Mrs. Gillco came running and took me into the house and put ice on my head. She then proceeded to call my mom and by the time my mom got there about forty-five minutes later I was still sobbing. They could not understand why I was still crying after forty-five minutes and when I was asked why I was still sobbing, I told them I was afraid they would not let me ride Thunder anymore. This is the sign of an up-and-coming horse crazy girl. I never let that deter me from riding nor did I let any of the other falls in my life stop me. Riding horses was my passion and would be for many years to come.

A few days later, up the driveway came a trailer with my pony in it. I spent the whole summer riding Thunder in the pasture while my mom worked in the garden. He taught me well how to ride. Unbeknownst to me that pony broke my nose that day he dumped me into that post and I had to have surgery many years later to correct it. So, I guess you could say that Mrs. Gillco was my worst teacher and my best teacher all in one.

MOVING TO CALIFORNIA

I started second grade at Delano elementary school, but before long I was told that my dad was to be stationed in San Diego, California. So off we went again on a big move to California. I was excited to see a new state and meet new friends. The trip to California was a long one. We made the trip in a station wagon with my mom and dad taking turns driving along with three kids. My sister, who was always crying, rode almost the whole three thousand miles on my mother's lap even while my mother drove. In the 70's there were no requirements for seat belts let alone baby car seats. My brother and I slept in the back of the station wagon. On our trip out to California we stopped one night at a hotel, this was a real treat because we generally drove straight through wherever we went. We were so excited because the motel had a pool and we could swim and have a good time after a long day in the car. We all got our suits on and ran to the pool; it was going to be so much fun! I remember my mother had a blue and white checked bathing suit with ruffles, she looked so pretty. She had to hold my sister because she was too little to swim by herself. My dad was with us too and he helped my brother and me; he let us jump from the edge and he would catch us in the air so we would not go under. We swam for a while and soon I was shaking. I was so cold I could not stand it so mom took me and got me dried off as I shivered and my teeth chattered with the cold. A little while later I was feeling horrible, I was achy, cold and I had a headache. We went to bed that night and when I woke up in the morning my glands were so swollen, I could not move. My mom took one look at me and discovered I had the mumps. We had a long way to go until we arrived in California and the trip was the most miserable, I have ever been on. We had to go through the mountains and as I lay in the back of the station wagon, I think I felt every bump along the way. Not to mention the altitude in the mountains and having swollen glands press against your eardrums, the pain was excruciating.

When we arrived in California, we needed to find a place to stay. Mom, Dad and three kids along with a cocker spaniel named Ginger; we found a kitchenette motel to rent by the week until we could find something else. There was a little swing set to play on and with my dog I set out to be a typical second grader. We stayed at the motel about two weeks, just long enough to find something else. Mom soon found an apartment to rent in El Cajon, this was a subdivision of San Diego, but we could not have a pet so we gave Ginger to an elderly man at the motel who fell in love with Ginger. He taught that little dog to fetch her brush and roll over so he could brush her belly and keep her well-groomed. I am sure she had a wonderful life, but I missed her terribly.

While I was in the apartment, I had a good time. There were kids to play with and every week a clown character would come and tell us bible stories. I had grown up listening to bible stories from my mom and grandma and I truly enjoyed that clown. Nowadays that probably would not happen just in case someone got offended because he was talking about Jesus. I do not recall how long we lived at the apartment but I am guessing not long. We attended a church in La Mesa, it was a church like the one we attended in Delano, with similar teachings. One weekend the church had a picnic in the mountains for all the families. This was going to be so much fun for all of us. We headed out one morning and when we got to the spot that the family day was going to be held, we piled out of the truck and ran to play. It was going to be great and they had a ton of food and games for the kids as well as for the adults. I remember the swings and people playing horseshoes. The adults were cooking bison meat in a pit for dinner and we were all excited to try it. Before long, I was not feeling very well and started running a fever. I went to our car and lay down and we left soon after. As you can see, I got sick frequently. When we arrived home, I went to bed. I had a bunk bed at the time and I slept on top. My mom brought me some Coca Cola, which was a treat; this must have meant I was sick to have such a treat. It was not long after that I started breaking out into spots. Yes, I had the Chicken Pox, soon after my brother and sister broke out with them as well. My brother and sister got them a lot worse than I did, I was not so miserable, but it was not much fun since I could not go out and play with my friends. My sister had them the worse, before long she was covered in those telltale spots. She had Chicken Pox in her ears, in her eyes and anywhere else you can get

Chicken Pox. Boy, was I glad I did not get them that bad. They were completely covered in calamine lotion; they looked like two little ghosts. Mom took a picture of them sitting on the couch they looked quite comical although I am sure they did not feel very well. It was not long after this that my mom and dad found a house to buy.

The house was in Santee, California. This suburb is about 30 miles east of San Diego. It was a quiet town with a lot of navy families because of the close distance to the base in San Diego.

LIFE IN CALIFORNIA

My sister was about two years old when we moved into our house in Santee. Our house was so beautiful, it was brand new and it had four bedrooms a kitchen and living room. We each got our own bedroom. Mom decorated our rooms; My sister's room was pink with pink roses and my brother's room was red, white, and blue and my room was yellow with yellow roses. My room was beautiful, it had matching wallpaper, and a comforter that my mom made, it was a beautiful room.

Because my sister cried a lot my mom took her to the doctor and had her tested for allergies. She was allergic to everything and she would not stop crying! The doctor told my mom that she could only eat white foods. This included applesauce, rice, lamb, and soy milk, yuck! When she turned two, we had a birthday party for her, but she could only have Rice Krispie Bars, so that is what we had for a cake. It was during this time that my mom had me join Pioneer Girls, it was a girl's group for church, it was like Brownies or Girl Scouts except you learned about Jesus and had a lot of fun with girls your own age. My mom took some of my friends along to Pioneer girls too. We always had a car full going to church at night. There was a lady down the street that had a neighborhood club called the "Good News Club." We met once a week and learned about Jesus and the Bible, both my friends and I had a lot of fun there. We also did arts and crafts, had snacks, and sang Bible songs. It was so much fun for all the neighborhood kids to get together at the home of this neighbor, I cannot remember her name, but maybe it will come to me.

My best friend I had in California was named Lila. She lived up the hill from us and she had a little brother. We played all the time and stayed overnight at each other's house a lot too. Her mom's name was Eden; I always thought that was a funny name. We played games in her room or we would roller skate. Sometimes her mom would say that she could not play because she had chores to do, this meant she had to do dishes. I would go and help her so she could get done faster and come and play. Her mom was very picky about those dishes and if they were not done just right, we had to do them over. We had the most fun together, just like two peas in a pod. Lila was a little older than me but in my same grade. She was very tall and thin just like her mother. Her dad was in the navy too, but he was a Captain. We had a park and playground just a few blocks away from our house that had a community swimming pool. Lila and I spent as much time as we could at that pool. It only cost twenty-five cents to swim all day! They also had a snack stand where we could buy candy, pop, and other snacks. It never failed that I would come home with a bright red nose and sunburned shoulders. My nose would peel in the summer until it would scab and bleed and my mom had to put white zinc oxide on my nose to keep it from burning any more. Of course, nobody knew about skin cancer back then, so other than the fact that it was painful we did not worry too much. Lila had two St. Bernard dogs and we would play with them all the time. We would pretend they were our ponies and ride them around the yard until her mother would tell us to leave those poor dogs alone.

One of our favorite things was to play with our Barbies. We would make Barbie clothes and dress our dolls. We had to use our imaginations back then for play because we did not have video games and we did not watch much TV. On occasion I would spend the night at Lila's we would watch TV with her mom.

Lila and I walked to school daily, but it was only about six blocks away. One afternoon, I had to walk home by myself. As I was walking, I heard this rattle, I was very terrified because I knew what that meant. There was a Rattle Snake nearby and I was scared to death of snakes. As I was walking, I glanced up the little hill by the sidewalk I was walking on and there in the flowers was the biggest rattler I had ever seen, not that I had seen any up to that point. I crossed to the other side of the road and walked way around. After that I was always on the lookout and always scared because you just never know where there might be another one.

We had two animals when we lived in Santee. We had a dog named "Dawg" and a kitty named "Kitty." We were very clever with names. Dawg was a cock-a-poo and kitty was a

Siamese. One day we were in the kitchen when kitty wanted to come in. My mom went over and let her in and discovered she had something in her mouth. Mom thought it was something dead and she went to retrieve it from kitty and low and behold it moved. It was a huge, hairy tarantula with eight great big hairy legs. My mom let out a scream that you could have heard for miles and kitty of course got scared and dropped that big thing right there in the kitchen. As it walked across the kitchen with its big hairy grotesque legs, my mom got a jar and captured it. Well, what can you do with a disgusting, hairy, gigantic spider in a jar? You spray with insecticide, so it dies and you send it to your grandma in Delano for her bug collection. I would have loved to be a little fly on her wall when grandma got this little gift in the mail and proceeded to open it up.

The one thing about California is it is always warm. We could play outside for endless hours; the highlight of the day is when the ice cream man came down the road. You would be playing and not paying attention at all, but when that truck came down the road with it is music playing, children would pour out of their houses from blocks around to buy ice cream from that man. He had anything a child could want from taffy to push-ups or rocket pops, they were wonderful. You could buy a great big piece of taffy for only ten cents! It was the highlight of the day if your mom gave you a bit of change to buy something from the ice cream man. Sometimes we would catch him on the way home from school and we would have a gooey snack to eat on the walk home. Living here was pretty much idyllic except for missing my grandparents. The 70's at that time in that place were safe and we never had to worry.

During our time in California my dad had two tours of duty. The first tour lasted about six months. This was not too bad; we would go once a month to the commissary (a commissary is like Walmart is today for people in the military) to buy groceries and they had a play area where we kids could play while our mom's shopped for groceries. Mom said this was the only break from kids she got was when we went to the commissary and she could put us in childcare while she shopped for groceries.

My mom met her best friend in California. My sister called her "Aunt Tootie" because she could not pronounce her name. She was married to a guy that worked on dad's ship and his name was Bob. My sister would go and stay with "Aunt Tootie." Because she did not have any children of her own, she loved having us come and visit her. She lived a little way away, but whenever my sister got mad at my mom, she would say she was going to run away to "Aunt Tooti's" house. She got mad frequently, she was a little spitfire to say the least.

The second tour of duty my dad was on while we were in California was supposed to last nine months. My mother kept getting letter after letter from my dad explaining that the tour had been extended. Of course, I was just a young girl and I did not understand why my mom would cry every time she would get those letters. I could not do anything to help her. At the time, the Vietnam war was ending, the POW's had been on TV being released and part of the bargain with North Vietnam the United States would stay behind and sweep the mines from the Haiphong Harbor. My dad's ship, the USS Ogden, was one of the ships chosen to complete this mission. So, for a long thirteen months my mom was a navy widow with three kids.

NEW FAMILY MEMBERS

While living in California, my mom got involved in the foster Child program. During this time, we had two foster kids. They were both teenage girls and the first one was Nelle, she was a cute girl with a turned-up nose, long straight blonde hair, and freckles. She shared a room with me. I thought it was so neat because she was older than me and I did not have to be the "big" sister anymore. The second girl that came to live with us was Dena. Dena was on the chubby side; she was around age 16 and to me she had to know everything. Both the girls were nice to me and I liked them very much. My mom loved to sew and she made matching shorts outfits for all of us girls with halter-tops. We looked pretty good in those outfits if I do say so myself.

Mom and dad bought a pick-up truck with a camper while we lived in Santee. This was a lot of fun. Sometimes Lila and I would spend the night in it and have it all to ourselves. We also had Aunt "Tootie" over one time and all of us slept in the camper in our driveway and we made popcorn and played cards, it was a lot of fun. The most fun though was taking the camper to the drive-in theatre; we could sit up in the top bunk and watch the movie. Usually, it was just me, my brother, Lila, and Nelle. Mom would make popcorn and we usually watched a Disney movie. This was a cheap activity for the family to do.

Occasionally we would go up camping in the mountains. It was a nice break from the city. One time while we were camping in the mountains, we were all hiking and of course out in the wilderness we did not have a bathroom. So, I told mom I had to go and she said go behind the bush. So I went over to this log that was crumbling apart, pulled down my pants and went to the bathroom. That did not seem as bad as I thought it would be although I was embarrassed to have to go potty outdoors. So on with our hike we went, as we returned to the camper, we were all tired and we decided to rest. But I just could not rest because occasionally, I would feel a tiny pinch in my pants. Starting with my legs, moving up to my behind pinch, pinch, and more pinching. I could not tell why I was feeling this way, maybe

I got into a poisonous plant while we were hiking. Finally, I got down off the top bunk and pulled my pants down, there on my legs and behind were little red fire ants and they were biting me all over. I screamed and danced around until my mom got them all off me. I truly know what it is like to have ants in your pants.

Mom got lonesome for grandma and grandpa so we decided one summer to take a trip back to Minnesota. Mom and dad had to get special permission from the County to take Nelle with us and they granted the permission. I do not know if Nelle had ever had a vacation, but it was fun. We drove the pickup and camper back to Minnesota and when we went through the desert, we were so hot with no air conditioning in the camper. Along with four kids and a dog we had to find a way to get cool. When you drive along the highway in the desert there are barrels full of water in case your car overheats so mom being ingenious decided to open dad's suitcase and get out white t-shirts for us all, including the dog. We would go by those barrels and stop and soak our t-shirts in water, put them back on get in the truck and drive until we could not stand it anymore and stop again. We managed to make it through the desert like this and were on our way to Minnesota.

When we arrived at grandma and grandpas, we were never so glad to get out of a vehicle. While at my grandparents we played badminton, horseshoes and went canoeing. We also did some target practice and my dad helped us girls shoot the gun. Everyone did fine except my sister, she was so tiny she could hardly hold the gun up. She would raise it and try to aim and as she rested her cheek on the stock the gun would slowly sink until it was pointed at the ground, we all laughed because she was so cute. Finally, my dad helped her so she could shoot it successfully. My siblings found out what it was like to be at the river house that summer. We had so much fun playing in the river, eating fresh corn out of the garden, and just spending quality time as a family.

My grandma and grandpa had a foster son whose name was Jason. He was not very nice though, he taught us things like blowing up frogs with fire crackers. I did not care for him because I did not like being cruel to animals. While we stayed there, we went fishing and Jason and I caught a walleye in the

Crow River. This was cool since all we ever caught was Bull Heads and Carp. One day I rode into town with my grandma and we went to the Coast-to-Coast store. My family knew the man that owned the store. His name was Jerry; he went to school and graduated with my mom. Well, I was so excited to tell someone about the Walleye we caught that I just blurted it right out to Jerry who was checking us out. Well, my grandma stomped on my toe and I was startled and asked her "why did you stomp on my toe?" Grandma was so embarrassed that I asked her that in front of Jerry and of course I had no idea that it was supposed to be a secret, so I was very confused. To find out later, she was worried there would be a lot of people that would want to fish out by their house if they heard of our one lone Walleye. To this day we laugh about that.

We worked in the garden, weeding, watering, and harvesting, it was truly a family affair. My grandma's brother also had a garden out by ours. My grandma's brother had mental illness that I did not understand at the time. He was paranoid schizophrenic and was fine when he took his medicine. One day he came out to the river house and was off his medication. He went out to the garden and started ranting and raving that we put salt on his garden to ruin it. He started pulling up his plants and throwing them and getting violent. My grandma had to call the sheriff to come and they took him away. I assume he went someplace to make sure he was calm and taking his medicine again, but I remember that day like it happened yesterday. It was quite scary. He had been in World War II and had a daughter who was schizophrenic. I felt bad for her she was so shy and when she came out, she never would say a thing.

We could not have a garden in California because we did not have the room, although my mom would plant a few tomatoes and we really appreciated the fresh vegetables out of grandma's garden. We stayed about a month at grandma and grandpa's and then we were headed back to California.

Lila and I were so glad to see each other again, it was a long summer with us separated for a whole month. Lila lived way up on a hill at the end of our cul-de-sac and she had one neighbor who lived right next door to her. His name was Bobby and he was awful. We did not like him, so we did not very often play with him, but one day we decided to play with him and as usual, he was being very mean. Well, lo and behold he had a broom in his hand and I guess I must have said the wrong thing and he shoved that broom right in my stomach and knocked the wind completely out of me. Let me tell you, that was the last time I played with him. I could never understand why kids were mean to other kids. Bullying at the time was not in our vocabulary, if someone was mean you just did not play with them anymore. I was always raised to be kind to people and to treat other's as I would want to be treated.

My mom belonged to a group of people that had Foster Kids, I suppose it was a support group of sorts but we would get our families together and do different things. One day we had tickets to go see the Minnesota North Stars play California in hockey. Boy was that fun; I had never been to a professional sports game before and of course Minnesota won. Being my heart was always in Minnesota that is who I had to root for. We also met a lady that had Foster Kids and she lived a little way away from us. One day she invited our family to come over to her house and I was very surprised to learn that she had horses. They were so beautiful and we got to have a ride on them. She even had a sorrel gelding that was so smart they taught him to kick a football. So, for a horse crazy girl, this was the place to go. I wanted to go there more often but mom said we had to be invited. I just could not understand why mom could not call her up and ask if we could come over.

Of course, being in California it was next to impossible to have a horse or pony. But one day Lila and I went to an outdoor church festival that was being held at our school. They had dunk tanks and bobbing for apples and all the fun things a church festival would have. But the best thing was they had two yearling ponies that they were raffling and boy did I want one. I ran home so fast, tore into the house and in my best out of breath voice I asked my mom if I could buy a raffle ticket. I thought if I could get a pony for fifty cents how could anyone say no? But guess what my mom said? No. I could not believe it, I was devastated. I did not understand why we could not have a pony if it only cost fifty cents. I had given it no thought as to how we would feed it or where we would put it. Our yard was about as big as a postage stamp but to me we had plenty of grass. What made this worse is the kids down at the end of our street won one of those ponies. So, all I could do is try to make good friends with those kids and maybe just maybe they would let me pet their pony. I got to see that wonderful pony occasionally but I think they caught on to the fact that I was trying to befriend them for their pony. I could not believe what lucky kids they were. Little did I know that I would soon have a pony of my own.

BACK TO MINNESOTA

Sometime in early 1975 my mom sent a letter to my grandma that said we were moving back to Minnesota. My dad was transferring to Chicago and would be commuting. My grandma and grandpa then went on the hunt for a house for us in Minnesota, they found 40 acres in Kingston with a house that needed a lot of fixing. It was built in the 1800's. The hardest part was leaving California and waving to my best friend Lila out the back window of our station wagon with tears streaming down my face because never again would I see my best friend.

We moved back to Delano and grandpa took his camper up to the farm in Kingston so we would have a place to stay. This house was not exactly what I was expecting. You see it was built in the 1800's and was log. It was a mess. There was no way we could live in this house until there was some major remodeling done. So, we lived in the camper, all four of us. It was cramped to say the least but at least it was summer so we spent a lot of time outdoors. Mom put in a garden and she spent the summer cleaning brush and working on the house. My brother, sister and I spent the summer living like Huck Finn, we played cowboys and Indians, climbed trees, and played tag among a few other games. We did not spend much time inside since it was either the old house or the camper. Believe it or not we only had an outhouse for a bathroom that summer, but it made it fun not to have to go inside to use the bathroom. It was only a one hole so only one person at a time could use the bathroom. Sometime during that summer, it was realized that we would not be able to stay there that first winter. So, in the fall of 1975 we moved back to Delano to stay with my grandparents. I was enrolled in Delano Middle School and I was beginning sixth grade. I loved school in Delano and my new teacher raised purebred Arabians. Her name was Mrs. Cane and she fed my curiosity about her horses if I got my work done. Since grandpa had a pasture for cows it was decided that at the age of twelve, I was to finally get a pony of my own! I was so excited I could hardly contain myself. Mom found an ad in the Delano Eagle for a pony and we went to look. She was beautiful, she was a black and white pinto pony named Cricket and she paced, which means the legs on each side strode at the same time, so she was very smooth to ride. We were able to purchase this pony for the grand total of twenty-five dollars and they threw in the saddle. My grandpa built a rack on the back of his pick-up truck and we could back it in the ditch and the pony could jump on the truck and be tied up front. Shiver's run down my spine when I think of hauling horses this way now. We took cricket home to grandpa's house and she was just a joy. We all took turns riding her and soon we got another surprise. My dad had bought a horse for my mom from the Marsden's family, her name was Sugarfoot. She was a beautiful black horse with a glistening coat, she reminded me of Black Beauty. Dad took mom over to Marsden's and mom rode that horse to grandpa's house, it was not very far and mostly on gravel roads. Madsen's were a family that we knew from church and I was friends with the two youngest children. I had grown up with them in church when we were in Minnesota. They also went to my school. We would get together either at their house or at our house and play. They were wonderful kids and the family was very dear to our family. My uncle was a best friend with Bill, one of their older sons. They had nine kids in the family, wow was that a big family. As a young girl, I had a crush on Danny, but we were just good friends. During the time at my grandmas, we went to the Delano Free Church where we went to Sunday School and about the age of 12, I rededicated my life to Jesus. Unfortunately, as you can see my walk with Jesus is an on again off again thing. I always felt that pull and even though I at times gave up on Jesus, he never gave up on me. Although I always believed in Jesus and I knew he died on the cross for my sins, it is just hard when you are not consistent with going to church. This is the way my life will go as you will see.

My grandma really tried to keep me involved in church and I was signed up to go to camp. I was nervous because I did not like going away from my family but I knew some people that would be there from church so I decided it would be fun. Our church camp is Camp Shamineau in Northern Minnesota near Motley. It is a beautiful lake setting with cabins for girls and cabins for boys. I also loved the fact that they had horses that we could go on trail rides during our free time. They had arts and crafts, church services and really good food! I was there a week and got a couple letters from home which helped a lot. I always enjoyed learning about Jesus and doing it in a fun environment was even better.

While in Delano, I met a girl in school who I would be good friends with for many years, her name was Linda and she liked horses as well as I did. She lived over near Marsden's and I would go to her house and spend the night and she would come over to my house and ride horse with me. She had neighbors next door who raised Morgan horses. Their name was common around the Morgan world. I thought their horses were the most beautiful horses I had seen, in fact Sugar Foot was a product of Marsden's pony and their stallion (oops!). Rob was in my class as well as a boy named Matthew. They used to shoot rubber bands at me to get my attention, but I was very uncomfortable around boys due to the sexual abuse I had suffered as a child. I was always fearful of them even though I am sure they meant no harm. They would always talk about things that made me uncomfortable so I tried to avoid them as much as possible.

When you have been sexually abused anything regarding sex can be a trigger.

Winter turned into spring and with the March thaw we started tapping maple trees at the river house. This was done every spring. We would drill a hole into the tree and place a wooden spiel into the tree. Then we would hang an ice cream pail on a nail below the spiel. When the days were warm and the nights were cool, the sap starts running. At least twice a day we would take sleds and five-gallon buckets out to collect the sap from the maple trees. Grandpa would build a fire up at the house and we would cook the sap down at a constant boil until it turned to maple syrup. We had to watch the syrup very carefully because it could burn if the fire is too hot. Mom and grandma canned the maple syrup, so that we would be able to have wonderful, sweet syrup on our pancakes and waffles and if we were lucky on fried corn meal mush. Harvesting maple syrup was a big job and everyone would pitch in, but it was worth it. Sometimes my mom would cook down the syrup further until it turned to sugar and we would have our own little cake of maple sugar, it was the best candy, it would just melt in your mouth and the flavor was terrific. I always felt like I was in Little House on the Prairie because a lot of what we did like tapping trees and making maple syrup was an art that not a lot of kids would see done, as well as living at the farm, working, and playing outdoors all day long.

After the maple syrup was finished at my grandparents in the spring we were again preparing to go to the farm. Mom suggested that we get a couple of animals for the farm that we could take in 4-H. I had started 4-H in Delano and would continue in Meeker County. My brother wanted a goat, so we went and found him a cute little doe named Lily (grandma at the club was not so fond of the name, since her name was Lilly). I was able to buy a little Jersey calf that I named Blossom. We had to bottle feed these babies and grandpa had an old van that was not useful anymore, so we turned it into a nursery. Those babies were quite a pair. When we moved to the farm the horses and my calf and Lily the goat went with us. My sister had gotten a little Banty chicken in kindergarten and she named her Patches. We really liked Patches, but unfortunately so did our dog and Patches was no more. We came home one day to a guilty looking dog and lots of feathers in grandma's basement.

Mom and dad finally got a bathroom in the farmhouse; yes, we had to use the outhouse that whole first summer! It was nice to be able to take a bath after playing outside all day instead of just washing up in a washbasin. We really roughed it that first summer. They started working on the upstairs and it was a slow process but we were able to live in the house mostly. There was a room upstairs that was so bad, it was full of bat droppings and I was completely terrified of bats. I totally avoided that room. We spent the summer at the farm playing, riding horse and being kids. In the fall we had to be enrolled in a new school. I was going to Litchfield Junior High I was going into seventh grade. I was excited because so far, I had never had trouble meeting people or making friends. I did make some friends at school. My best friend at the time was Rita, she had horses and lived on a farm too. My other friend was Bonnie, she lived in town but was just as horse crazy as the rest of us. We spent time at each other's house although to be fair I spent more time at Rita's house than she spent at mine. She also had a couple of sisters that we hung out with at her farm. We would ride all over the area, there was a little town names Manannah and there was a real cute boy that lived there so we would ride past his house just to try and see him. Mind you we were to chicken to talk to him but we giggled and laughed all the way home as we rode through the field roads and gravel roads. One time we had a great idea. We got on their big quarter horse named Maude and while she was walking across the barn, we were going to grab onto the rafters that went across the top of the barn. Now picture this Rita was in front, followed by me and then Rosa. Rita managed to grab a rafter and so did I but Rose missed hers and I ended up knocking her off the horse and she fell to the ground. We were so worried because she kept crying and we did not know what was wrong so we took her to the house and her parents had to drive her to the emergency room. When they got home poor Renee had a broken arm. So, we got in a little bit of trouble for those shenanigans but not too bad. My dad was gone all the time and she had such wonderful parents. I loved going there and spending time. Her dad always helped us with the horses and would go trail riding with us. They had some purebred Arabians and to say the least I was a bit envious. We did not have a church at this time but I would go with friends if they went.

I was not prepared for what I was going to encounter at that school or on the bus. We were very poor during those days and going to a new school was very difficult, I was bullied daily. My bus ride to school was an hour long in one direction and the kids on the bus were very mean. I had never been teased or made fun of before this; I had always been a happy little girl and did not understand why I was being targeted in such a way. During that time, I had hand me down clothes and because of our situation on the farm and being a preteen, I had trouble with keeping my hair looking clean; back then we did not shower every day like they do today. I have very fine hair and overnight it would look dirty, I would get teased and tormented by these kids daily not only emotionally, but physically as well. There were a few that would never let up. It was a daily occurrence for me to get off the bus crying and of course back then nobody talked about bullying and there really was not anything my mother could do; I do not know if she even knew about it. I look back and wonder if I would have had a better self-esteem if I would not have fallen prey to these kids and their tormenting. I wonder where Jesus was when I was in such pain. In today's world this would have been brought to the school and people would have probably been expelled. I do not know, but I do know that it shaped my life and affected me forever. I always feel uncomfortable around peers my own age and I feel it was because of this time of my life. I never thought to leave it in God's hands because he seemed so far away. I was in such a constant state of depression when I went to school, I saw a counselor. It never really helped because the kids never let up! The kids that were the worst of the bunch came from homes that were broken. I do not know if berating someone else made them feel more powerful. I often wonder what they think when they look back on their younger years and I wonder if they wish they would have treated me differently or if they even remember how mean they were. I am in my 50's and still remember the tormenting that was bestowed upon me. I still wonder where God was during this time and why he would let this happen to someone who loved him.

PRINCESS AND BLOSSOM

About this time, I was ready for a bigger horse and decided I wanted to buy one with my own money. I had sixty dollars saved from babysitting and mom and I went to the Hutchinson Horse Sale to see what they had. When I was there, I fell in love with a little two-year-old filly that looked like she had come from an abusive situation. She was nothing but skin and bones and her hair was matted and she had no life in her eyes. She came into the ring loose and of course we did not have a lot of experience with horses to know that loose horses that come into the ring probably should be avoided. Well, I had my money in my pocket and I was going to save that little filly. I bid and bought her for sixty dollars. Then the fun started. We had no idea how we would get her home; she was not halter broken and we did not have a trailer. We found a guy that had a cattle truck at the sale and paid him to bring her home. Well, it took four men to get a halter on the poor scared little thing. They cornered her in the stock truck and put the halter on her. We brought her home and we encountered another problem. Horses are really scared of pigs. The reason they are terrified of pigs is because pigs are related to bears and they carry that smell. Of course, horses are fight or flight animals, but they prefer to run, so we did not dare get this little filly anywhere close to our hogs. So being the tom boy my mom was, she decided we should tie her between two apple trees in the front yard and the next day my mom worked and built a fence around this filly. I had to come up with a name for her and I chose, Princess. I was infatuated at the time with Princess Ann of Britain because of her equestrian abilities so I thought that was an appropriate name for a little filly. She was so scared I could hardly get near her. I would bring her oats and apples and give her hay and before long we had made fast friends. I guess you could say we were sort of alike. I was kind of a little ragamuffin and so was she. I felt like she understood me and I always could tell her anything. She was my best friend and my confidante, just what a girl of thirteen needs. I broke Princess out, but not in a way that most people would, I think I just spent so much time with her she trusted me to do anything. I started out bareback and before you knew it, I was riding that filly all over the country! I felt free when I was on her. There is nothing in the world like flying down a hay field with the wind blowing your hair and not a care in the world. This is what I lived for at the time. I would ride to my grandparent's farm that was about six miles from my house and ride all around their property. About this time, I was starting to notice boys and right across the road from my grandparent's farm were the nine farm boys! And they were cute! Of course, they did not notice me, I was a skinny little freckle faced kid that did nothing but ride around on my horse while they had to work hard on their farm.

My best friend Rita started going to horse shows with her horses and I thought I would like to do that but we did not have a trailer at the time. Well, that was not going to stop me, I just rode to my grandparents and spent the night and then rode the mile or two to Kimball where they quite often had horse shows. Of course, I did not have a clue as to what you were supposed to do at a horse show, but it did not stop me from trying. I learned little by little about showing, got frustrated, and tried again and again. I had a bit more success at the County Fair in Litchfield Minnesota. The summer of 1977 we were in the 4-H club in Kingston, my projects were mainly my cow and my horse. Blossom was freshening (having a calf) that summer so we kept a close eye on her. The whole neighborhood was waiting for that calf. One afternoon I was out front with Blossom and her water broke. I ran to get mom and phone the neighbors and we all got to see that little calf be born. She was a little heifer and I named her Brandy, she was the smooth soft brown of a pint of brandy. In 4-H we do a farm tour; this is where we go out to everyone's house and see his or her 4-H projects. It is a chance for us to show off our work and get advice from another 4-Her. Well, I was quite a hit that summer because my cow had recently calved. Blossom was a Jersey Cow and they are known for their rich milk. If you fill a quart jar with Blossom's milk you would end up with about three quarters of it filled with cream. So, using her ingenuity my mom made homemade ice cream for everyone in the club. We each got a wonderful ice cream cone when they came to my house. I was very proud because I felt like I fit in for once.

My brother and I went to the Meeker County Fair that year and I brought Princess and Blossom and her calf, Brandy. My brother brought Lilly his goat. I showed Blossom and won reserve champion with her and a State Fair trip. I also competed with her in showmanship and it did not go very well. My grooming was spotless, we had a neighbor that showed cows and came over to help me prepare Blossom. She showed me how to clip a cow and polish their hooves and because Blossom had horns, we had to take a piece of cut glass and scrape her horns to get them smooth. After we did this, we had to take very fine sand paper and rub those horns until they shone. Right before we were to show her, we were instructed to put oil on her horns and they would be black and shiny. I was all prepared for showmanship and I entered the arena just the way I was taught and got about half way across the arena and Blossom decided she had had enough of showing for one day and right in the middle of my class she laid down. I was completely embarrassed. I pulled her tail, pushed her, and pulled the lead shank and to no avail that darn cow was just going to lie there and chew her cud. Finally, after a little more coaxing she got up. She was all dirty and by then my showmanship class was finished so that was kind of a wash. I also showed Princess and did well, I did get a red in showmanship because she was too thin. I rode her too much and she did not have a chance to put on any weight. I did not win a state trip with her but I won some money. I also won the hunter over fences class, since Princess was so brave and we jumped obstacles all the time, a two-and-a-half-foot jump was nothing for us. Later I took her out back and bet some boys that I could beat them at a race with Princess against their bigger horses. We lined up at the starting line and my little Princess was off the starting line and halfway down to the light pole where we were to turn around before those big horses could even get going. After word got out, nobody would bet me anymore so my cash cow dried up. We had fun, Princess and I, no matter what we did we were a team. I can honestly say that in those days Princess literally saved my life. I know now that depression was to be a part of my life and Princess allowed me to be myself. I did not know it at the time but I think God placed that little mare in my care to give me a best friend. I needed that at the time.

Of course, mom took pictures of us at the fair and afterwards she had the film developed. We laughed and laughed when we got those pictures back because she had the camera backwards and all we got was old farmers, chewing and spitting their snuff sitting behind her.

One of the favorite things I did living in Kingston was ride Princess with friends to the lake, we would swim with the horses at the boat landing, jump off their backs and go as far as hang on their tails and let them pull us in. I am sure we were not very popular with the lake people when they had horse apples (manure) floating up onto their lawns, but of course kids do not think of those things, and they frankly do not care! That fall I went to the Minnesota State Fair with Blossom for 4-H. I had fun and met some cool kids that seemed to really like me. Blossom did not come from a dairy farm so she had never been milked with a milking machine. We milked her at home by hand twice a day. While at the state fair I took her to the milking machine because being a teenager, I was lazy and did not want to hand milk her. The person overlooking the milking really did not want to put the machine on Blossom because she had not been trained and a lot of times, they get scared and kick and act up. But Blossom was so sweet, I convinced them to try it and she just stood there like she had been milked with a machine her whole life. After she was milked, I took her back to her stall and gave her graham crackers, one of her favorites. It is funny how something as sweet as a cow can be so important in one's life.

ROUGHING IT

That summer my mom and dad decided to buy a couple of heifers. One was a Hereford or white-faced heifer and one was a polled Shorthorn. Heifers are generally not the easiest animals to have around and we had a corral by our barn that we figured they would be safe in. So, we brought those heifers home and put them into the corral and within about five minutes those blasted heifers had jumped the fence and were headed down the road. Well mom jumped in the truck and went to get them, after about an hour of chasing those darn things, she got them rounded up and brought them back, tied to the bumper of the truck. So, being the "farmers," we were we decided to tie a tire around their neck, so that it would prevent them from jumping over the fence. Well needless to say that lasted about another five minutes and they were running down the driveway with tires around their necks. The neighbors called and said that they saw two red heifers running down the road with tires around their necks and were wondering if they were ours. Once again, my mom and dad had to chase those blasted cows down the road and through the fields. After rounding them up one more time, they put them back in the corral and tied cement blocks around their necks, well this is surely going to work my mom said! Guess what that white faced heifer did it again, although she was much slower this time and when she got over the fence my dad jumped on that cement block to hold it down and the heifer just pulled him down the driveway. My dad probably weighed 150 pounds soaking wet so he was not much of a detriment to that cow. We obviously were learning the hard way the pitfalls of farming.

We had neighbor's right next door in Kingston who raised hogs as well. We always helped each other out when one of us needed an extra hand. It was time for them to bring sows into the barn for farrowing (farrowing is when they give birth) and they asked if we would come over and help. Sows can be the most difficult things to work with and they truly have a mind of their own, so it helps to have several people when you need to move them. We would stand in a line with wooden pieces of plywood that had a handle in the top so we could guide the sows in the direction we wanted them to go. That was the idea here, you wanted to go in the direction of the barn. So, we were all in a line and I did not have a piece of plywood so they told me to stand and wave my arms to deter the sow from coming my way. If you know anything about those old sows you know that if they see the tiniest amount of daylight that is exactly where they are going to head. We started moving the sows toward the barn and this one sow, she was the color of butterscotch pudding, decided to make a break for it and she ran straight for me. I was not scared of them I just whooped and hollered trying to turn that sow back toward the barn, but she had other ideas. She headed straight for between my legs and just like that I fell over the top of her and was having the ride of my life! I was laughing so hard; I could not stop and when I finally fell off everyone was in hysterics laughing at the crazy picture I had just made. We would have made a crazy sit com for TV about that time.

Another time we were at our neighbors to help them clean slabs. Slab cleaning is when they scrape the pig waste off the slab. It is generally liquid manure. So, my mom and dad had a great idea and were going to play a trick on me. They picked me up by my arms and legs and swung me as though they were going to throw me into this pit. My dad did not quite get the joke and he let go. In a split second my mom and I both landed square in that pit of hog manure. We were both covered from head to toe, it was so disgusting, we could not go into the neighbor's house and take a shower and we could not get in a vehicle to go home. So, we went up to the old porch while my neighbor held up an old sheet. We stripped off our clothes and had to be hosed down. Of course, everyone else thought it was hilarious. My first thought was going to school the next day and smelling like hog manure. If you know anything about hog manure you know that the smell does not readily come out of your hair or clothes. I think I took about six baths that night and I think I still went to school smelling like that manure pit. Just what a young teenage girl wants to go to school smelling hog manure especially if you do not fit in in the first place.

We stayed the winter at the farm and it was cold. There was not a lot of insulation in that house and we heated it with a cook stove and an old oil-burning stove. We had my cousins out from the cities to spend the weekend and my mom was always able to make things special and fun. We had taken some of the field corn we grew and ground it up to make corn meal. We could eat that corn meal in a mush like Malta-Meal or we could cook it down and refrigerate it, slice, and fry it and serve it with maple syrup. Either way it was delicious! My city cousins did not think they wanted to try any of that stuff until my mom convinced them that way back when that is what the Indians ate and then they were all for it. We had fun that winter; we had a great sliding hill in the back pasture that was always great. We would spend hours out there and come back to the house for a steaming cup of hot cocoa to warm up. We also had a pond in the back that we could ice skate on. What more could a kid want?

One night, when it was incredibly cold, I think it was about -20° and our oil heater ran out of fuel. I woke up to frost on my blankets and we were frozen. Mom and dad went out to start the truck and let it warm up and they bundled all us kids up and we went to my grandparent's farm in Kimball. I think for my mom that was about the last straw. A person can only work so hard, without something going their way. Unfortunately, my mom was doing this mostly by herself since we were not much help and my dad was gone with the navy to Chicago most of the time.

As I said before, my dad was an alcoholic, which I did not know at the time because my mom was always careful to keep these things from us kids. He never could keep a job and we never had any money. It was inevitable that my parents would divorce. My mom stuck it out for thirteen years, which is a lot longer than I think I could have handled all the responsibility of three children and no money. My mom came to my grandma's where we kids were staying to tell us that she was getting a divorce. It was the beginning of my eighth-grade year and I was so embarrassed and worried because I did not know anyone in 1978 that had been divorced. How was I going to tell my friends, especially Rita who came from such a wonderful home? I think this is when I started to rebel. Even though I was just thirteen years old, I was already sick of my life. We had trouble enough without this and even though I never felt close to my dad, he still was my dad and I was afraid of the consequences of my mother's decision. I think then I was desperate for love and knowing what I know today, I knew I could use sex in place of love. I think a lot of little girls learn that when they have been sexually abused. Of course, this was not in my realm of thinking at the time. At the time I just wanted feel love and I did not think of the consequences like most kids. One evening I went down by the lake to see a boy that I liked and he was older than myself, he took me to a party and my mom did not know where I was and she called my grandpa. The party we went to was mostly adults and they were all drinking. I did not drink and they dropped me off at the end of the driveway. My grandpa was so mad and he gave me one of my first ever spankings and I did deserve it. This was the beginning of my rebellious years.

During the eighth grade I had my first boyfriend and his name was Marshall. He was very cute with dark hair and dark brown eyes, and we dated for a few months. Now I look back on it and it really was not dating, we saw each other in school and held hands at the football games and that was about it. Sometimes we would talk on the phone, but not often because it was long distance. Most boys then were obnoxious and drove me crazy. It is funny the things boys will do to get your attention, like tease and cajole. I could never understand why they would do that when it would have been so much better if they would have talked to me like a normal person would. But when you are young that is the natural progression of things. The funniest thing happened when I was "going" with Marshall. His best friend Robby also liked me and one night at one of our football games, those two got in a fight over me, it was so stupid it was hilarious. I decided I was not going to be a part of that anymore and left them fighting on the football field. School activities were few and far between because we lived twenty miles from school, so the only way I could go to school activities was if I was staying at a friend's house in town.

I could tell mom was unhappy, being out at the farm alone and struggling with three kids. My father lived in St. Cloud, but could not hold a job and did not pay child support. My mother was dependent on AFDC and with three kids that surely did not go far. She was also lonely; she had spent the better part of her life alone and when my dad was around, she was still the responsible one.

Soon it was apparent that our financial situation was in dire straits and that we had to do something. I took Princess to a sale, along with Sugarfoot. We ended up selling Sugarfoot, but Princess did not bring the money I thought she should, so I talked a couple of guys that I knew at the sale barn to hall her home for me. A little flirting got me a long way in those days. They thought if they did this for me, they would end up with a date. I of course had a different idea. I let them have a kiss or two, but that was the extent of it. I guess I learned early that you can get a lot out of a guy if they are interested in you. These guys were a lot older than I was, I was 14 at the time and they were 18 or 19. They brought my horse home; I jumped out of the truck, thanked them, and went into the house. Boy, were they disappointed, but it did not stop them from the pursuit, every time they saw me at a sale, they would try and try to get me to go out with them. They were too old for me and there was no way I was going to go out with them! Frankly, I was a little scared of them.

I ended up selling Princess to a couple of girls that lived on a dairy farm between Kingston and Litchfield. I warned them that they needed to get the tin out of their pasture because horses were not like cows. They did not heed my warning and it was not more than a week and Princess was down at the University of Minnesota getting her hoof reattached. Blossom and Brandy were also sold. Blossom went to South Dakota along with Brandy. I did make good money when I sold these animals, but it was also a sad day for me. I was very attached to them. People ask me how I can just sell one of my animals today and I think it is because I do not let myself get really attached to them. My thoughts are everything is for sale when you live on a farm.

DECEPTION

I know my mom was concerned with our living situation and how we would spend the long winter in the log house. I think she was desperate to make sure that we had a warm place to live and plenty of food to eat because she met a man that she soon married that I would describe as evil. He put on a good face in front of other people and had us fooled.

This man had an appearance of being a good provider, nice all-around guy and that he liked us kids. He had a good job as a draftsman and made good money. He was a little like the imperviable wolf in sheep's clothing. My mom and Harry got married around Christmas time 1978, they went to South Dakota to get married and we stayed with our neighbors in Kingston. We put together a small reception for them when they got back and life looked like it was going to be fine once again.

We moved to Cokato where Harry and his son Harry, Jr. lived in a small house just North of Cokato. Things started out fine, we all got along and Harry seemed like a nice guy. He allowed me to have a couple of ferrets I got from a friend at Dassel Cokato High School and I got a new horse with the money from selling Princess and Blossom. My sister got a couple of ponies from Harry's dad and she had a ball with them. She named one Flicka and we dressed her up in pajamas and entered her in the pet parade in Cokato. The new horse I got was a purebred Arabian; I had high hopes for this horse. He was the purebred Arabian I had been longing for. We went down to a farm and saw Ham. He was a rose grey two-year-old that had just been started. I fell in love with him and made the deal. They delivered him to my house with pink ribbons in his mane and tail. Little did I know that this horse was a total knot head! He was so hyper you could hardly do anything with him and no amount of riding could wear that gelding down. I think he would have made an awesome endurance horse. I suppose I should have known that he did not get enough exercise at this house. The land was too small to have a horse on.

While I lived in Cokato, I found a wonderful job in Dassel. I worked at a horse farm that raised Polish Arabians. This job was a perfect fit for me, I went there after school and cleaned stalls, exercised horses and sometimes I even got to ride. I would get off the bus have a snack that Mrs. O'Riley always left for me, change my clothes and head to the barn. They had the most beautiful horses and I was in my glory working there. They also gave lessons and worked with other people and their horses. After I got a job there, I bought lessons for my sister's birthday so she could learn to ride. They trusted me to work their stallion, Mako*. He was an import from Poland and quite valuable. One time Mrs. O'Riley told me to sweat Mako*, which meant that you put a neck sweat on them and work them until they are lathered. It helps to thin down their necks. I lunged him, and in the past had seen them wash Mako* down in the wash rack after to rinse the salt off. So, I thought I was doing the right thing by putting Mako* into the wash stall and rinsing him off. Mrs. O'Keefe came into the barn and was shocked to see her stallion completely soaked. It was not warm at the time and unbeknownst to me I was only supposed to rinse his neck, not his whole body. Well, I never saw Mrs. O'Riley get so mad because she was afraid her prize stallion would get sick. In the end everything turned out o.k. and she told me not to worry about it, but not to do it again. I was relieved because I would have felt horrible if anything would have happened to him.

In the fall the Arabian Horse Association held a show down in St. Paul at the state fairgrounds and the O'Riley's were taking down a filly that they had imported from Poland. This filly was worth a tremendous amount of money and she was very nervous. I had taken care of this filly and she knew me so I told Mrs. O'Riley that I would ride in the trailer with the filly and keep her company so she would not be scared. It seemed like a long trip down there, but she arrived safe and sound without a problem. This show was huge and there were many futurities and a lot of people came from all over the United States. If your horse finished his championship at this show people would throw a party in celebration of this achievement. They had champagne flowing as well as food. Nobody watched teenagers that well and I met a couple of guys there that I hung out with. We drank quite a bit of champagne and got quite tipsy. I ended up sleeping in the trailer that night and the next day we went back home. The boy I met at that show wrote to me and had a crush on me, he rode bulls for High School Rodeo and he sent me pictures of him riding those bulls. He was nice, but I really was not interested in him. I did learn that I liked the way I felt when I drank. I could forget everything in my past and just be relaxed.

I started Dassel Cokato High School as a ninth grader. I had a difficult time making friends by now and the people that befriended me were not the best for me. I got into drinking, smoking, and doing drugs with these people. I was destined to get into trouble. I started dating a boy from DC, his name was Aaron. He was always kind to me and I felt very important since he was a senior at high school. He even gave me his class ring to wear. I do not know why he would want to go out with a freshman but he did. We hung out a lot, went to some parties and had great times roller-skating at the skating rink in Cokato. The skating rink was made from an old chicken or turkey barn and it was 'the' hangout for us kids back then. My mom or Harry would drop me off at the roller rink and if we did not want to stay there a bunch of us kids would head out in someone else's car and go to a party or make one of our own. Then when it was time to get picked up, we would be at the rink just as planned.

As we got a little older, we sometimes went into Cokato and had French fries and cokes at the Norseman restaurant. This was a favorite hangout late at night for us teenagers, if you had money.

One weekend I decided it would be a good idea to have a party at the house since my mom and Harry were away. A few of my friends came over, along with Aaron, my boyfriend, and we were having a good time. Then someone mentioned a party out in the country and I was tired of my little brother and sister spying on us so we left and went to this party. To tell you the truth I do not remember much about the party because I was drinking quite a bit. I do remember the party was outside and I was drinking Sloe Gin. Everybody was drunk and Aaron did not want to leave, so he asked a guy he knew to drive me home. I only know the guy's nickname was "Crispy" if that tells you anything. He was into drugs from what I had heard from others. But I needed to get home because I had left my young brother and sister home alone and I was supposed to be watching them.

"Crispy" was nineteen at the time (I was fourteen) halfway home he pulled over and started kissing me; I was very drunk and had no control over myself. He continued and had sex with me. Some would not call it rape, but I learned later that what he did would be considered rape. He was an adult and I was too drunk to say no. This was my first time and I barely remember it. I walked up the driveway after he dropped me off, with tears streaming down my face, I still had to clean up the house after the party and my sister helped me. She knew something was wrong, but never brought it up. She was too young to understand anyway. I was so scared after that I would become pregnant. But how could I tell anyone, after all I felt responsible since I was intoxicated. I never even told Aaron my boyfriend at the time. The shame I felt was just added on to the guilt I felt growing up. After that my drinking and smoking amped up, I suppose to try and forget although I did not think like that. I just wanted to forget everything in my life. I wanted a normal life like I had when I was little.

Harry's drinking seemed to be getting worse, he would drink every night and when he drank his personality would change, he started getting very threatening and I really hated it at his house. My mom and Harry would fight and yell; I could not help but hear them when I was upstairs. I just wanted to get out of there. He also yelled at me and called me names, things I had never heard of before. He would accuse me of listening in on their fights when I could not help it, it was a very small house and he was very loud. One night he was so out of control and I heard him hit my mom. The next morning, I woke to find my mom with a black eye. She was stuck with no way out. She had no money of her own and did not even own a car. I never dreamed we would be in this situation. I just spent my time away as much as I could. I took off to a girlfriend's house because of the tension at our house. Unfortunately, I never thought about my siblings having to stay there. I was only able to take care of myself.

My drinking, smoking, and using got even worse. Aaron and I broke up and I started hanging around a worse set of people if that is possible. One night I told my mom I was staying at my friend's house and she told her mom she was staying at my house and our plan was to stay out all night and party. We started out at my new boyfriend's house. I never seemed to have trouble finding a new guy. We drank quite a bit at his house until his mom came home and kicked us all out. His mom was supposed to be gone all weekend and his mom showed up and busted up the party. My friend and I went to another party in town, it was a couple of guys, they were adults and had their own apartment, remember we were only 14 or 15 at the time. We smoked a little pot and were listening to music when the neighbors called the police and filed a noise complaint. The police came knocking at the door and because we were minors the guys told us to go sit in the bedroom so we would not get caught. We were drunk and had been smoking pot so the last thing we wanted to do was get caught by the cops. They were smarter than we thought because they checked the bedroom where my friend and I were hiding and found us. They put us in the cop car and hauled us downtown. I was being so disrespectful to the police officers and at the time I could not care less. My mom and Harry got a call about five thirty in the morning to come and get me. I can tell you my mom was not happy! She lectured me and grounded me and all the while I was being a smart aleck to her. I was so miserable at that house but nobody could see it. My life was falling apart and I could see no way out. The worst thing happened after that incident. My mom told me I could no longer work for Mrs. O'Riley. I was devastated by this news because I loved that job. It was the only thing that truly mattered to me at the time. Life went on and we lived in the minefield called home. Not knowing when things would blow up again. Some days were good, but most were devastating. Obviously, you can see I had totally given up on God being in my life, I never gave him a thought.

One night on my fifteenth birthday, Harry came home with a fifth of sloe gin and gave it to me as a birthday present. Harry was an alcoholic and I guess he wanted company. I proceeded to drink that fifth and drank almost half of it. I got so drunk I had to be helped up the stairs, but drinking and doing drugs was my way out, even if temporary of that horrible situation. I always relished the calm that came with drinking and doing drugs. I would hide marijuana in my bedroom and sneak out into the barn to smoke. My life was falling to pieces, bit by bit and to get a reprieve if only for a few hours using drugs and alcohol was the only way out at the time.

Aaron and I tried to get back together one more time and he picked me up and took me to the Meeker County Fair, we had a nice time walking around the fair and I really like him. I think he loved me, but of course at the time I was probably way too young for him, since there was three years separating us. I do not remember seeing Aaron after this last date. Not long after this my situation got worse at home. Harry had made threats to me including the fact that he wanted to rape me to show my mom what kind of a person I really was. He also threatened to shoot me and he had guns in his possession, so the threat was taken seriously. My mother had no choice but get me out of that house. I realize now that she did it to protect me, but at the time all I could think of was that she was choosing Harry over me. I felt so abandoned at the time but did not know how to express myself.

FOSTER CARE

As foster homes go, I got lucky our old neighbors said they would take me in on their farm. So, I went back to Litchfield High School, although it was quite different for me this time, I was a sophomore in high school. The friends that I had when I was there in junior high wanted nothing to do with me now; I was depressed, lonely and hated my life. I knew at my foster parents I was safe, but I missed my mom every day. I would go to school and come home, but it all seemed so mechanical. I was a loner at school and I started skipping classes and taking diet pills and No-doze for the energy they gave me. I sometimes wonder if these pills contributed to my heart problems later.

I liked the farm life and I liked the fact that my horse came with me. I went to church with my foster mom in Kimball and was a part of the youth group, but my heart really was not in it. Sometime that year we got a call from my foster mom's aunt. Her son Daniel, had stolen their pickup truck and a gun and was going to kill himself. I knew him and his brother; they were close to my age and would come out and ride horse with me sometimes. My foster mom had a horse as well named Cherokee so we would ride together. I was very worried about Daniel, but really did not think he would do anything. Maybe it was just a cry for help. But I soon learned that he drove to Duluth and went to the lighthouse. The Sheriff talked to Daniel's parents then flew them to Duluth. They told the authorities to wait for them that maybe they could talk to Daniel and get him to come out. The authorities did not wait and Daniel shot himself and he died. I was sick and at the same time I wished I had that kind of courage. Being dead had to better than life, I hated my life and at the time all I could see was that Daniel did not have to deal with life anymore. I was sad that he died and really did not have anyone to talk to about it, so I just closed-up and kept everything to myself. The only thing that kept me from committing suicide was my belief in God and the belief I would not go to heaven.

That fall I recall being down at the State fairgrounds, I believe it was for a youth conference for church. I remember getting a phone call that my horse had been shot. I was so worried about Ham and was told the story of what happened. He was grazing in the front of our farm in the ditch and a couple of boy's joy riding, came by and shot him in the rump with buck shot. He ran down the road with blood streaming down his rump. I could never understand how someone could be so cruel to an animal. They never did find out who did it. Ham was physically o.k. but he had buckshot in his rump that you could feel after that.

During that fall conference I met a guy at that youth group that was very nice. He was older and a counselor and his name was Miles. He wanted to see me and I would have liked to see him as well. We kept in touch for a while and he invited me down to the cities to meet his parents. He was a nice Christian guy and he probably would have been someone I should have gone out with, but because of my fear of older guys I told him I could not come down there. I was afraid that he would expect something out of me that I was not ready for. Later, I moved back to my mom's house and he even came up and took us swimming.

My foster parents always tried to make me feel like part of the family, but of course I just wanted to be with my mom. My mom and grandparents were also not on speaking terms at the time. My grandma did not approve of divorce and they quit talking after a huge fight they had over my mom's divorce. My mom gave strict instructions to my foster parents that I was not to see my grandparents. This broke my heart because my grandparents were very special to me. One day I was outside at the farm and they drove by slowly and waved but could not come and talk to me. I was heartbroken because I missed everyone so much. I could not understand why I could not have just gone to live with my grandparents.

My mom took me to Buffalo to see a counselor while I was in foster care. He was a robust gentleman with pitch-black hair. In my mind I was afraid of him. I did not like men that had dark hair, except my grandpa, because my uncle that abused me had black hair. Harry came to one of our sessions and told this counselor that I was belligerent. I was so mad. I cannot believe he would say how bad I was when he was such a horrible person. Counseling at the time did me no good, I was not diagnosed with depression and I did not like this counselor. I would probably have done much better with a woman counselor considering all the sexual abuse I had been through. But to be fair nobody knew about the sexual abuse so they would not think about what type of counselor to get. I kept the secret well from the rest of my family.

I enjoyed the farm, but it was a lot of work. I helped after school, with chores. I took care of the pigs, watering, feeding, and cleaning up after them. My specialty if you could call it that was taking care of the piglets after they were born. I would cut their teeth and tails and dip their umbilical cords in iodine to prevent infection. It sounds horrible, but it must be done. We clip their needle teeth because they are so sharp, they can tear a sow's udder and we clip their tails because as pigs get older sometimes, they want to chew on the other pig's tails. This prevents infection in the older pigs. I was also good at giving shots and taking care of quite a bit of the veterinary work around the farm. The time with the animals was when I felt the most at peace. Ham kept me busy and we rode quite a bit. He lived in their abandoned old house that was to be torn down. It was quite a sight to see a horse looking out the living room window of that old house.

I also did a lot of cooking at their house because I happen to be a pretty good cook. Even at the age of fifteen, I did quite well in that department. I never minded cooking, especially in the winter when it was cold outside. The guys also appreciated my cooking and I think my foster mom liked not having to oversee that department. The year at my foster parent's seem kind of a blur to me and my memories are not as sharp as I would like them. During that year in school, I had no friends, I was so lonely and could not understand why my old friend Rita would not be friends with me anymore. She tried out for cheerleading and hung out with a totally different crowd than she used to. At the end of the year my life was kind of a mess and soon I was to move again. My mom finally broke free from Harry. My foster family sold her a cheap car for about one hundred and fifty dollars and Harry's sister and brother-in-law rented us a house out in the country up near New London in a little town called Hawick.

Because of my drug and alcohol use, I went into drug and alcohol treatment at the St. Cloud Hospital (I should have gone to a psychiatric program). I worked very hard at trying to overcome some of the things that had happened to me in the past. I talked with counselors about the sexual abuse from my uncle, but I still do not think people knew quite how to deal with those issues yet. My dad showed up one day while I was in treatment. This was a surprise because I had not seen him more than once or twice since him and my mom had divorced in three years. He just could not handle being around us kids; I think he felt guilty for not being in our lives. He told me he came specifically to tell me something. He told me that he was not my real father, that my mother had me before they were together. This came as a shock to me, not that I had a very good relationship with him anyway, but I always assumed that I was his, even though I was born before they got married. When I asked my mom about this she was disgusted and told me that I knew that anyway. I did not know it and I was mad at her for not telling me herself and then making it appear as though I knew it all along. So of course, this was another thing I had to deal with in treatment.

During treatment I met a friend named Barry, he had attempted suicide and we hit it off as friends. He introduced me to his brother. After I was through with treatment and moved back out to Hawick, I went on a few dates with Barry's brother. He was a very nice guy, once again a few years older than me, but he was a gentleman. He invited me to the Coborn's picnic, his dad worked for Coborn's in Clearwater as a manager and they had a company picnic. We went to the picnic and then went to a movie. We were very good friends. He came out to Hawick and we went swimming with my brother and sister over at Lake Koronis one afternoon. My brother and sister did not get to do too much so they had a great time. He played the drums and we remained friends but it did not seem to be right for us to date. I learned later that he was diagnosed with Multiple Sclerosis and was wheel chair bound. He later passed away. I really felt bad that I did not go to his funeral.

HAWICK

I started school that fall in New London-Spicer and met one of my best friends there. Her name was Shannon. She was into horses as much as I was and we hit it off right away. She worked for a veterinarian in Spicer and did chores and such at his horse farm. She also had a couple of horse at her parent's house. She was dating a guy she met from Willmar, his name was Evan. He worked at an auto detailer in Willmar where one of his friends worked. His friend's name was James. Shannon wanted to set me up with James on a blind date, but I was not too interested in a blind date so we drove to Willmar and did a little scoping out. I thought he was cute and he wanted to meet me so we decided that we would meet Evan and James at the grocery store where Shannon worked after she got off. Shannon came out and got me at the house, as I did not yet drive and we drove back to Spicer. When we got there, we could see James and Evan hanging outside their truck waiting for us. James was so shy he wore his hat (which I soon came to learn he never took

111

off) pulled low over his eyes because he could hardly bring himself to look at me. I had never met someone who was so shy.

I was disgusted and told Kim that I would not go out with a guy that could not even look at me. She was just as confused as I was. So, this meeting did not go as well as she and Evan would have liked. What I did not know at the time was that James was indeed impressed with me and when asked by Evan if he thought I was cute, he did not have to say much, the smile on his face said it all. I thought that was hysterical but it did not exactly encourage me to go out with him. Shannon said he wanted to go out with me and I told her that I would go out with him, but under no certain terms would I go out with him unless he could get up the courage, pick up the phone, call me and ask me out. I was trying hard to be grown up about dating. I had learned some things about myself in treatment and had a little more self-respect.

It did not take long for my phone to ring. It was James and he asked me if I would go out with him. I said yes. James and Evan were into cars and were building a stock car in the garage where they worked. My friend Shannon and I spent a lot of time at that garage watching them work on that stock car. We would go to stock car races and watch Evan race. James built the motor and kept it running for Evan. We went to movies and parties together, in fact the first rated R movie that I had ever seen was Friday the Thirteenth. It was terrifying and I think James had fingernail marks on his arms for days after seeing that movie. Little did I know it but I was falling for that guy!

I managed to get James a job doing bodywork on my grandpa's Black Chevy truck. James was thrilled to have a side income and my grandpa was happy to give him some business. We would get together and work on that truck. I thought that truck was so cool. James did such a good job that he was able to get other work. My grandpa got the truck fixed up and sold it. James reminded me a lot of my grandpa; he was ambitious and was not afraid of hard work. I think my grandpa and James could relate and because he was so like my grandpa, I fell in love.

My mom went into treatment after I did for co-dependency. She had arranged for a girl that was about nineteen to stay with me and my brother and sister while she was gone for thirty days.

The girl she hired lasted less than a week and then I was responsible for the house, chores, my brother and sister, laundry, and meals. I was a junior in high school and was responsible for everything at home as well as getting myself to school. Because I did not drive, I was stuck as far as going to the laundry mat and the grocery store. If it was not for James, I would not have been able to handle that month. I managed to get the kids to school and get to school myself without missing very much. I was a whiz in the kitchen so cooking was not a problem and James spent many evenings over at my house eating. It was the least I could do since he was helping me by driving me the places I needed to go.

My sister, brother and I would go once a week up to see mom in treatment for family night. We got a ride from another family that was traveling up to St. Cloud for family night. Family night is where you spent time in a group therapy setting with the person that was in treatment. We were able to discuss things that bothered us and they could tell us what they were feeling as well. One evening my mom asked me to bring her up her leather coat and her cigarettes. I remembered her coat and forgot her cigarettes. I had so much to remember for someone that was as young as I was that the cigarettes just slipped my mind. When I arrived on the unit to see my mom, she just got so angry because I had forgotten her cigarettes and she was yelling at me. A counselor stepped in and told her that it was not my fault and that she should not yell at me. I felt terrible that I had forgotten one of the things she asked me to bring and I still feel bad about that. Mom changed a lot after she had gone through treatment. In treatment when you are co-dependent you are taught to be more independent and take care of yourself, although my mother took this literally and she decided it was time for her to have a life.

My mom spent a lot of weekends with the kids in St. Cloud visiting Huck her new boyfriend. He was nice but I did not like the fact that she was always gone. Huck had an older son that was into photography so one sunny day when I was in St. Cloud, he asked me if I would go out to our Hawick farm and take some pictures. I said sure, I would be happy to. I enjoyed being photographed and he did some very interesting pictures. I was in shorts and a ruffled top and he did some pictures by the old barn door and some out in the field by an old stove that was dumped out there. I never got to see the pictures but I was told they turned out very nice. I was very photogenic when I was younger and was thrilled to be asked to be a subject in his pictures.

I spent most of my weekends with James. The one thing I did like was that I pretty much ran my own life. I quit drinking after treatment and was doing well in school. I went out for the fall play and won a part playing an old lady. It was quite fun even though I would get very nervous. Everyone including my grandparents came to watch me in the play. I met a boy that I knew in high school that wanted to go out with mem his name was Randy. He was the homecoming king and the quarterback on our football team so I was quite thrilled that he had taken a liking to me. I was still going with James at the time so I only went out after play practice one night, but it amounted to nothing since I was already seeing James.

I decided that maybe I should go out with different guys just because I had not done that very much. I called James on the phone and told him that I thought maybe we should see other people. He was so upset he came out to our house and made the trip in twenty minutes from Willmar to Hawick. That was fast! He said he did not want to break up and I backed down and said O.K. I guess I did the right the right thing considering what the future was to hold for me.

Mom was obviously still struggling financially since she received no resources from my father. So, that Thanksgiving a neighbor who managed a turkey farm gave us a huge live turkey for our Thanksgiving dinner. I think it weighed about twenty-seven pounds. We were very grateful. My mom had butchered chickens before, but nothing this big. She had a great idea; she put this big tom turkey into a gunnysack with a hole cut into it for the turkey's head. She hung it up from the rafters in the barn and took a knife and cut its head off. This turkey took to flapping and before long she was covered in turkey blood. She ran to the house and before she could get the water boiling to dip the turkey in and take the feathers off, she heard a knock on the door. She opened the door and was covered head to toe with blood while holding a butcher knife. It was a UPS man looking for the neighbor and he had a look of sheer shock on his face.

When he asked if this was the neighbor's house my mom had wished she would have said, "it used to be." But of course, she explained that she was butchering a turkey and that the neighbor lived a little farther down the road.

We lived in Hawick for the rest of the school year and I dated James that whole year. I fell in love with him. He was very sweet and cute too! He had brown hair and blue eyes. Everyone thought we made a cute couple. He was a senior at Willmar High School and I was in my junior year at New London Spicer. In the spring of 1981, I got the influenza. I was very sick with a high fever, cough, and chills. This illness then moved into my lungs and I got pneumonia. I was sick in bed for six weeks. I had picked out my prom dress for my junior prom. It was beautiful. It was pink and lacy and had a scoop neck bodice with lace. I was going to pay on it a little at a time by babysitting. After I got sick, I knew that I could not get that dress and of course my mom could not afford it so I just figured I would be staying home from prom my junior year.

One night as I lay on the couch feeling miserable, James who had been visiting me faithfully showed up with a dress bag with my prom dress in it. He had gone and taken his own money and paid for my dress so I could go to prom after all. I had never had anyone be this kind to me other than family. I started back to school after five weeks off, but was still so weak I ended up going home and missing another week. My teacher in German was so mad that I was not in class and he was not very understanding. I finished that quarter of school on the B honor roll even with being so sick.

While I was at the end of my recovery, James came out with his truck and asked if I wanted to road trip out west to Ortonville. I honestly do not remember why we would drive out to Ortonville but I went along. He had a case of beer in the back of the truck and he drank the whole way. I was still quite ill and I ended up sleeping with my head on his lap the whole way there. I do not think I was too interesting but I guess it was better than hanging out by himself. We hung out a lot like this. Sometimes we would go fishing or he would go hunting and I would ride along. Usually if he went hunting, I would stay in the vehicle and wait for him, I would bring along a book to read or a crossword puzzle.

James and I went to both our proms. Mine was held in Willmar at the Kandi Entertainment Center Ballroom. We had a pretty good time. They had good food, it was Chicken Kiev, and a dance, but we all pretty much left to go party after we ate. James' prom was held at his school. They had a grand march and we had to go to his parent's house to have pictures taken. James bought me a corsage for both proms. At his school they had a grand march where we all had to walk over a bridge and have our picture's taken and then inside, they had their prom in the gymnasium. We went in for a little while, but we all had reserved rooms at the motel on Highway 71. James and I and some of his friends including Mark and his girlfriend went to the hotel and partied. It was quite a night. We were all up most of the night and went home sometime in the morning. By that time James and I were an official couple.

We went to a party at Evan's one night where this girl from my school was hitting on James, he was drunk and did not seem to do much to thwart the advances of this girl. I was so mad when I came into the living room and saw her sitting on his lap and him doing absolutely nothing! So, what did I do, I went and sat on Evan's lap just to show him that two could play at that game. Of course, he did not like that, so that pretty much woke him up out of his fog and we left the party together. We argued about it a little bit, but I guess it was not as big a deal as I thought it was at the time. Other than that incident, we never really argued a whole lot as a young couple.

My friend Shannon broke up with Evan, I can totally understand why, he was not exactly a catch. She stayed single for quite a while. Shannon graduated early from New London-Spicer high school and I had to finish out the year by myself. That was very hard since we always did everything together, including skipping occasionally to go to Willmar. It was kind of our tradition to go to Taco Johns in Willmar on Tuesday's when they had Taco Tuesday and get two soft-shell tacos and a medium Pepsi. We would usually end up skipping school and did this a few times over the year. She even would come and pick me up at school when she was finished so we could hang out. It did not seem to affect my grades in school, as I was able to keep up a B average throughout my junior year.

It was not long before my mom informed me that we were going to move again. I was devastated since I finally found a place that I fit in. Mom had bought a house in Clearwater and wanted to move there since she had friends in St. Cloud and the surrounding area. I was so angry and I told her I was not going to another school. I would quit first. We talked to my counselor at New London-Spicer and they agreed that since I only had two credits left, I could get them at night from area learning center and during the day I would enroll in St. Cloud Vocational School. This worked out well because James was enrolled in parts merchandising in Willmar Vocational School and we would graduate at the same time. James and I agreed we would continue to see each other and we would take turns driving back and forth on the weekend to one another's house. I sold my horse before the move, which only made sense since I spent very little time with him anyhow and before long, we were in Clearwater.

CLEARWATER

We moved during the summer, between my junior and senior year in high school. I was sixteen and turning seventeen. My grandma and grandpa asked me if I wanted to get my graduation pictures taken for my graduation present and I was thrilled. I had just assumed I would not have graduation pictures done. My mom could not afford them and I did not have a job yet. Grandma arranged for me to come to Delano and go to Linda Motsko's photography to get my pictures done. My mom's friend from California had moved in with us after she divorced her husband and I was able to borrow clothes from her for my graduation pictures. They turned out very nice and Linda Motsko even asked if she could use one of my pictures in the Delano Eagle for her advertising. I was thrilled that she would do that. It really made me feel important.

Living with mom and "Tootie" in that house was not easy; instead of having one mom I had two, which I did not appreciate very much. I got a job out at a YMCA day camp and drove mom's car out there to work. I worked the entire summer and earned five hundred dollars to buy a car. James found me a sound; solid car that he said would be good for me. It was a 1970 Monte Carlo, with a 350 big block Chevy engine. It was green, so not my favorite color, but it did the job. It got me where I needed to go and James could work on it for me. I started at the vocational school and was taking bookkeeping. I really did not know what I wanted to do but had to pick something. I applied for financial aid and received enough to put me through the nine-month program at the vocational school. I had enough for gas and books as well as my tuition. I would put twenty dollars' worth of gas in that car every Monday and it would get me through the week of school. I have not seen 99 cent gas in a very long time! Generally, James would come to see me. He had bought a van with a bed in the back and we spent many weekends together in that van. We even got in a bit of trouble in that van. One weekend we were down by the dam in

Clearwater and a sheriff knocked on the van door and asked me if my mother knew where I was. Well, she did and he did not have much to say after that. I was lucky, I could have gotten in a lot more trouble than I did in that van if you know what I mean. My mother did know where I was.

One Thursday night James' parents called me and said they do not know what to do with him. He had gone out and stolen tires from a business in Willmar, along with Evan. They were going to put them on their stock car. James' parents did not know what to do with him and I suggested they let him sit in jail. I never condoned stealing and was disgusted with him that he would do such a thing. His parents had had more trouble than just that with him, but this was the last straw. I told them if they would quit bailing him out, he probably would learn a lesson so that is what they did. They let him sit a whole weekend in jail. When he called me to tell me he could not come that weekend I was so mad at him I told him that while he was sitting in jail that I would be going out and having a good time. Of course, that did not happen because I really did not have friends in Clearwater but I guess it did not hurt him to think that was what

I was doing. That was the last time James got in trouble. Later he wanted to get into the Air Force and they would not take him because of his record. I know that this really disappointed him, but unfortunately sometimes we must pay the price for our decisions we made in the past, and sometimes we do not.

James and I continued to see each other throughout that winter. One weekend we went to Alexandria to watch to snowmobile races and spend the weekend together. We rented a room in Alexandria and had a wonderful weekend. We spent some time at the mall and even looked at engagement rings. I was in a hurry to get married because I wanted to be in control of my life and be able to get out of the living situation I was in. We had a great time in Alexandria; we drank hot Dr. Pepper for the first time and just enjoyed being young. My home life was once again deteriorating and I was ready to get out.

Mom had started dating a guy from Fergus Falls and her friend "Tootie" was dating his brother. They were nice guys, but they were alcoholics. Mom loved music and they would spend a lot of time at our house playing music and partying. Some mornings we would wake up to drunken men that were friends of the guys lying on the living room floor. We would have to step over them to go to school in the morning, after they had played music until one or two in the morning.

This was a difficult time and I hated the fact that my mom was getting involved with an alcoholic once again. My uncle Jon was living with us at the time as well, which made me very uncomfortable. Of course, my mom did not know about the sexual abuse between him and me so it is understandable that she would ask him if he wanted to stay here. He was working in St. Cloud at a Park and Recreation Department. We had a house full with Mom's friend "Tootie" living there as well her son and then there was myself, my brother and sister. I had a room in the basement and James would spend the weekends there. Nobody had a problem with James sleeping with me which as a parent I cannot really understand. I think that everyone thought that I was older than I was. I am not saying that I would not have snuck away or slept with James in the van or anywhere else, I know I would have, but the fact that I slept with a boy under my mom's roof is unbelievable to me now as a parent.

One weekend my mom went up to her boyfriend's parent's house in Fergus Falls. He had a very musical family and of course my mom loved music. My mom's friend was to be at home with us. On Saturday evening I got a call from my grandparents that my great grandpa at the Club had passed away. Naturally I was upset and wanted to call my mom. When I went to make the phone call, my mom's friend said I was not to call my mom because it would ruin her weekend. I was so mad I could have spit nails. Who was she to tell me I could not call my mom and tell her about her grandpa's death. Once again, I saw that my mom's good time had to come before the family and we were left to fend for ourselves and grieve without my mother there.

One week at the vocational school they had snow daze. During this week there were different things on different days. For instance, they had a slave auction. This entailed each class would pick someone to represent them and people would bid on them and the class who raised the most money would win a prize. I was nominated to represent our bookkeeping class. The student senate which I was also a part of set this auction up in the cafeteria. We would stand on top of a table and then young adults would bid and whoever won the bid would get the slave for a day, it worked like an auction. On that day I dressed nicer than usual, with tight jeans, boots, and a black shirt. I did my makeup and my hair better than normal so that hopefully we could win the prize. Soon it was my turn to get up on the table and the bids started. There was this cute guy that was bidding, he looked like Grizzly Adams if you remember him. Soon the bids were above $75 and I knew so far that was the highest bid so we were in the running for the prize. Can you picture this nowadays! I am sure it would not be allowed. The bids kept coming and before I knew it, it hit $150 and finally stopped! It was not the cute guy that won the bid. The guy that won was a computer nerd but of course they would have the money. Look at Bill Gates! So, I spent the day with this guy, carrying his books and following him around. Oh, and we won the prize for the most money raised.

February was just around the corner and what girl of seventeen would not be thrilled to have Valentines Day coming up. I was and was thrilled to be able to spend it with James. Valentines Day fell on a Friday that year and I was waiting James to come. He always took off from school and drove up on Friday night to spend the weekend with me. I ate supper and was watching out the window for him, of course in those days we did not have cell phones to call someone and let them know you are coming. So, I just watched out the window and it was getting dark and I was getting very worried. He was never this late. The later it got the more concerned I got until about nine o'clock he pulled into the driveway. I was so relieved that nothing had happened to him but so mad because he did not call me and tell me he was going to be late. I did not say anything to him because I generally did not like confrontation so I usually kept my feelings to myself. James came in and sat down as if nothing was out of the ordinary and we watched some TV. It was not long and he said he had to get something out of the van, so he went out and got a flower for me. I thought this was my Valentines Day present, which was understandable since we were both in school and had bills to pay. James did have a job still at the auto detailers that he worked during the week. Soon he gave me another present and told me to open it up. It was an engagement ring. I was so thrilled. We had looked at engagement rings when we went to the snow mobile races in Alexandria but I never dreamed he would drive there and buy it. That was why he was so late; he got off school, drove all the way to Alexandria to buy my engagement ring then drove all the way to Clearwater. We were going to get married. I was thrilled beyond belief. We still had to finish school, but life was just getting started for me in my eyes.

MARRIED LIFE

I graduated from high school and vocational school at the same time in June of 1982. I was 17 years old, about to turn 18. I received my diploma from high school in the mail and I went to the graduation ceremony for vocational school where I sang a duet with a girl in my class for the ceremony. James also graduated that spring and we finally could get on with our lives, together. We rented an apartment in Waite Park; it was a small apartment with one bedroom a living room, kitchen, and bath. But it was our first place together, so we liked it and it was cheap! We lived above an old couple that needed some help, so James would help and do a few things for them in exchange for cheaper rent. It worked out very well for our first place.

James found a job right away in St. Cloud, he was going to work for Tenvoorde Ford as a night parts man. He worked from noon until closing which was nine at night. I got a job at a waterbed warehouse as a collection's agent. I was not exactly cut out for collections, but at the time I needed a job. I met a girl at that job named Mandy and she had horses, so I had someone to visit with while I was on my breaks. My boss had a Porsche and he asked me if I wanted to go for a ride in it. I said sure because I had never been in such an expensive car. He drove around a while and showed me the power that car had in it. I had a good time and thought I was doing well but like I said I was not cut out for collections and I was let go.

James and I were planning our wedding; well mostly it was me planning the wedding. We had decided on the date of October 23rd 1982. I do not know why we decided on this date since it was pheasant hunting opener and he would always go hunting on our anniversary, but at the time it sounded like a good date. I had met a girl that was dating my uncle, her name was Cathy. She did not date my uncle very long and started dating a guy that was to become her husband. She found out she was pregnant and they decided to get married. I asked Cathy if she would stand up for James and me and be my matron of honor. James had met a guy from school in Willmar, his name was Kenny and he stood up for him. While we were planning our wedding that summer, my grandpa had a van that he wanted bodywork done on. We parked the van at my mom's house because we lived in a small apartment and there was not anyplace to work on it in Waite Park. One day we went out to the house to work on the van and it was gone. So instead of working on the van we drove the motorcycle down to my grandparents in Delano and dropped off something James had borrowed from my grandpa. Well, my grandparents asked us why we were not working on the van, because they knew that was what our plan was and we told them that mom had taken it for the weekend. They were very mad because my mom had not asked to use it. When mom got back my grandparents chewed her out for taking the van and then she got very angry with me and said that I had tattled on her to my grandparents. This was not true, I just answered their questions, and I never would have just volunteered the information. I was hurt because she was the one in the wrong and she put the blame on me for something she did. After that we did not speak for quite some time, my mom did not come to my bridal shower or my wedding.

I found a beautiful dress in an antique shop that I purchased for fifty dollars; it was tea length and a 1950's style. We were on a budget so we could not spend a lot of money on this wedding, but I still wanted it to be memorable. I found a veil that matched the dress at a garage sale and James borrowed a suit from my uncle. My great Aunt helped with the reception, we had it in the church basement, and she served little tea sandwiches and hors d'oeuvres along with punch, coffee, and cake. I bought my cake at Cold Spring Bakery; it was lovely, done in shades of orange for fall. My uncle's wife was working as a photography assistant and we had our pictures done for free. After the wedding we went out to get in James' car, it was a 1971 Monte Carlo and was decorated by Cathy, Kenny, and James' brother. We all decided to go out after the wedding and we met at a little bar near where James and I were going to spend our wedding night. It was a nice night and a nice wedding, but I missed having my mother there. We spent one night in a hotel and then we went back to the apartment. I did not mind; I knew we could not afford a honeymoon and I was happy just to be married and starting my life with James. Of course, being a young girl of eighteen, I had the dream of 'happily ever after' like most young women when they marry.

James went back to work and our life continued. About six months after the wedding, I found out I was pregnant. We were still living in the apartment and we knew that we would have to move because it was not big enough for three. I am not sure if James was excited about the pregnancy or not, I know that I was. It is hard to describe the feeling of finding out you are going to be a mother. I know I was excited and I do not think I gave it an ounce of thought that this was going to be a big responsibility. I think it was a little like playing house at the time. Well, it would not take long for reality to set in.

BABY BRIANNA

My grandma and grandpa had bought a house in Clear Lake to remodel and rent out. Just about the time we were looking for a bigger place, they offered to rent this house to us. It was bigger all right. It was an old farmhouse with three bedrooms up and one bedroom down. It had five and half acres and James and I were excited to be able to have a place out in the country, maybe I could even get another horse. We moved out to Clear Lake in May or June; I was barely pregnant but looking forward to the future. It is funny how we always look to the future and if we knew what the future held, we might just spend more time appreciating the time we have. I was working at the Travel Plaza in Clearwater, waitressing and James was still at Tenvoorde's. He was such a good worker; they would never let him go. It seemed like a long time until our baby was to arrive, but I spent it fixing things up and going to garage sales. James's parents gave us a crib that had been James and we seemed to manage somehow.   We were so broke; we lived from paycheck to paycheck and at times hardly had anything to eat.   I think we lived on Campbell's soup and macaroni and cheese that winter. I know that it was a stress for James to be so responsible at such a young age; we were only eighteen and nineteen at the time. We did not know if we were going to have a boy or a girl and my foster mom was going to wait until after the baby was born to have a baby shower.

That winter was very cold and a hard winter, we had to use our fuel oil sparingly and kept the heat turned down as low as we could stand it.   We did not go out, but spent a lot of time watching movies on the VCR or watching TV when the weather was bad.   I quit working when it got to tiring and stayed home to wait for our baby that was due January 21st.   I saw a doctor in Sauk Rapids, he was a general practitioner, and I never had any pregnancy problems and did not expect to have any delivery problems either.   As my due date came and went, I was miserable and did not have many contractions until one very snowy night.   We were in the middle of a snowstorm and my mom suggested that we come over to "Tootie's" house and wait out the storm in Clearwater. It would be easier she said to get on interstate 94 to go to the hospital if the baby was going to come. I had contractions that night pretty much every ten minutes or so and we finally decided to go to the hospital before the weather got bad, I was about a week over due. At the hospital I was terrified, I had obviously never had a baby and when I got on the maternity ward, I could hear women screaming in pain. This made me more nervous. They checked me out and I spent the night walking the halls, but in the morning, I had made no progress so they sent me home. I went back to the doctor and he thought I probably did not know when I got pregnant. That was typical of a male doctor in those times to think that a woman could not possibly be smart enough to know when she got pregnant and of course being young I did not feel confident enough to argue with him. We went home and waited and waited and waited until finally, three weeks after my due date I was told to go to the hospital that they would induce me.

We went to the hospital bags packed and ready to come home with a beautiful little baby! But not so quick, this baby was not in any way shape or form wanting to come into this world. I was put on a drug called Pitocin. It would start my contractions in earnest and it would not be long before I had our little bundle of joy. I spent the next twenty-seven and a half hours in hard labor because when you are induced your labor is very severe. I was getting very tired and my blood pressure was going up. The doctor came in and checked me for dilation and effacement and when I got upset and told him it hurt, he told me to quit being such a baby. Can you imagine after I had been in labor for so long! I was so mad; he is lucky I did not give him a big old kick in the chops. The doctors and nurses finally decided to do an x-ray to see how big my pelvis was because they could see the top of the baby's head but she just would not come down any further. After the x-ray the doctor thought I could still deliver the baby. They called in an obstetrician since I was having so much trouble and after pushing for two and a half hours, my blood pressure skyrocketing and I was going into shock, they decided they needed to do an emergency C-section. I told them I did not care how they got this baby out of me just get it out! I was terrified and in so much pain. The nurses instructed me not to push anymore which is like telling someone not to breath because sometimes you just do not have any control over your body.

My mom called grandma and grandpa to come and it was a horribly foggy night, it took them quite a while to get to the hospital, but they managed to make it before our little baby was born. Before surgery they told James that it would take about ten minutes and he would have his baby to hold and after about a half an hour the nurse told him that they had trouble, the baby was stuck in my pelvis and they had to push her back up into the uterus and then take her and I hemorrhaged while they were performing the c-section. They brought the baby up to James in a blue blanket, so he assumed it was a boy and they said oh no, she is a girl; we needed the extra blankets because of the temperature in the operating room.

When I woke up a little from the anesthesia, they brought me in my bed to the nursery on the way back to my room. I was expecting this little rosy baby that looked like the pictures of the Gerber baby and they showed me this little baby that had two swollen eyes and was black and blue. I started crying because I thought she looked so ugly, I could not believe I had done all that work for this little homely baby. Then I promptly fell back to sleep. Of course she looked bad, she had been through a horrible ordeal trying to be born and after I woke up, I was thrilled to have my little girl. I do not think I ever saw James's smile as much as he did that day, he was so proud to be a daddy and proud of his little girl.

We had to come up with a name and I liked Brianna because it went good with Brandon. I knew a horse farm in Willmar with a similar name. I liked the way that went together, so that is what we named her. We took her middle name from the horse farm, so her name was to be Brianna Lee. She weighed in at 8lbs 13oz. and we were lucky that she made it into this world. I spent a week in the hospital and then finally went home.

I had never really heard of postpartum depression, but I soon found out that it is a real illness. I had a beautiful baby a wonderful husband and I was so depressed; I could not get out of bed. Nobody really saw that I was having trouble and I never felt like harming my child like some women go through but it was all I could do to feed and change the baby and then go back to bed. I felt so guilty that I could not be the mother I wanted to be. I never felt like I bonded with Brianna when she was a baby. I went through the first year of her life in a stupor. Brianna was such a good baby and it was a blessing to have her.

GRANDPA

One afternoon before James went to work, I got a call that my grandpa had had a massive heart attack while he was setting monuments in Princeton, Minnesota and was in the hospital in the same town. We were told we should get there as soon as possible. We took Brianna next door to Angel and James and I rode the motorcycle as fast as we could to the Princeton Hospital. There in ICU my grandfather, who had always been the strength of the family, was lying in bed hooked up too many tubes. He needed to be stabilized before he could be moved, but would eventually be sent to HCMC for a triple bypass. I guess we should not have been surprised that he would have a heart attack with the heavy work he did and the fact that he smoked and never watched the way he ate. But never the less, it was a shocker for the whole family.

It was not long when James came home and said that he had gotten a job offer in Atwater at the Ford dealership and he wanted to move. So, I thought maybe a move was what we needed. We packed up and moved all our belongings to a little town called Kandiyohi. We rented a house there that had three bedrooms, a kitchen, and a nice living room. It was a rambler and I liked the fact that it was so nice. The rent was reasonable and it was very close to work for James. The one thing I did not know is that it was very drafty, the house did not have proper insulation, but we put up plastic on the windows and we lived there for about six months. Brianna would have her first birthday in Kandiyohi. I wanted to have a nice little party for her and I bought a sheet cake and invited the family over, including the grandmas and grandpas. My mom had made Brianna a little table and chairs so we put her in that to eat her cake, but first I wanted a picture. I got the camera and Brianna went to touch the cake with her chubby little fingers and I said 'don't' before I even thought about what I was doing. Well of course this startled her and she cried and I felt terrible. I still get teased about 'yelling' at the baby when she just wanted to touch her cake. Brianna had her first accident at the house in Kandiyohi, she was in her walker in the kitchen while I was baking and I did not realize she had gone over to the doorway to the basement. The next thing I know she was tumbling down the stairs and I was in a panic! I ran down the stairs to get her and God had to be watching because James had thrown his hunting clothes down at the bottom of those stairs and she landed on his down vest. The only mark on her was a little scratch on her forehead from the zipper of his vest. I was so relieved but knew I had to watch her better after that.

I was a stay-at-home mom and I liked it. James got another job at the International Truck dealership in Willmar and we moved again out to a little house on Garage Road. Brianna had her kitty JP that stood for Jemima Popovich and it was not long before I got the horse bug again. I went out to Hawick where there was an Arabian farm and talked to the lady and before I knew it James agreed to let me buy a 2-year-old filly for $500 dollars. We had about two acres behind our house and a little shed to keep her in so it worked out perfect. Of course, with a baby I did not have a lot of time to work with her but when James was home, I had a hobby that I could work on.

My filly's name was Anata and she had the sweetest temperament. I took her to a couple of shows, but mostly just spent time with her at home. One afternoon as I was looking out the back window at her and she started running and I noticed there was a collie chasing her. She ran through the fence and was loose. I had to try and catch her with a baby on my hip. I was so angry that someone let their dog out and it ran my horse through the fence. We caught her and everything was O.K., but at the time I was terrified. The neighbor apologized and said they would watch him better from now on.

Living in Willmar was O.K., but I missed my family. Brianna was coming up on two years old when at Thanksgiving time we had a huge snowstorm. I was called and told that once again my grandpa was in the hospital. I was so panicked because my grandpa was the only male in my life that had always been there for me. Once again, James drove me down to the cities to HCMC and we found out that my grandfather had been diagnosed with leukemia. They started chemotherapy at once and he was soon in remission. Our family was so thrilled that they were able to stop this horrible disease, but it did not last long because he was only in remission a short time and he was again battling for his life.

We lost my grandfather in April to leukemia and the family was devastated. He was very young, only 60 years old and no longer would I have my grandpa to spend birthdays with or to be my strength and someone to lean on. The funeral was held in Delano and I stayed with my grandmother during the funeral. Brianna was two and she happened to get the stomach flu during the funeral preparations. One night we woke up to her throwing up violently and had to rush her to Waconia hospital with dehydration. I was exhausted and stressed out, how do I choose between my baby and being at my grandfather's funeral. At the hospital the nurses said that Brianna needed to stay at the hospital for a few days and they admitted her. I was so torn about what to do but the nurses and my mother made the decision for me. They said that they would take good care of Brianna and that I needed to go say goodbye to my grandfather. This was one of the hardest things I had ever done; leave my baby in the hands of strangers. We got through the visitation and we were able to get Brianna right after the funeral. Grandpa was buried in the Delano cemetery; I was hysterical and just hugged the casket and did not want to say goodbye. When the monument was set, all the grandkids placed their handprints in the cement at grandpa's headstone. I wonder how he would have liked that when he was so meticulous about his cement work. I tend to believe that the grandkids would have taken precedence over neat cement.

BACK TO CLEAR LAKE

Things went back to normal after grandpa's death. James had a job offer back at Tenvoorde Ford for more money, so we moved back to Clear Lake and bought the house we previously had rented from my grandmother. I was fortunate enough to get a call that the girl who had bought my horse Princess was selling her and wanted to know if I wanted her back! That was easy, yes! I went and picked her up and brought her home. One of the first days I had her I wanted to see what she remembered, so I set up barrels and went to run a pattern. She always cut the barrel close, but I never hit them. That day she cut it too close and I hit my knee on the barrel. Boy did it hurt, but I did not think much of it, I put her up and went in the house because I had to sleep before my shift at the Travel Plaza. I lay down and my knee throbbed and before I knew it, it was double the size and I had to go to ER. I tore ligaments in my knee and had to be on crutches for a month! Well at least I had my favorite horse back even if I could not ride for a while.

James and I worked hard and made our payments, it was not easy, we struggled with money and James and I had a tumultuous relationship. He could be very moody and unappreciative of what I did at home. I felt I was not important to him and was very dissatisfied and with my past I went back to old behaviors. I had always had a low self-esteem and it did not help for someone to remind me of my downfalls and failings. I was bound to break at some point and it came soon.

The county fair was in Howard Lake and my mom took a bus down to the fair so we could stay in it. I took my horse down to the fair to show. I was looking forward to the show but I met a guy that had horses and we connected. I ended up having a one-night stand with this guy, not something I was proud of but if I am being truthful, I must add everything into this memoir. My guilt was horrendous and I ended up telling James what I had done, he was so mad, he even had a 12-gauge shotgun out and I was terrified he would use it. I ran to the neighbors and ended up going to St. Cloud Hospital for treatment, I felt it was a better choice than the psychiatric ward even though that is probably where I should have been. I believe I never got better after having Post Partum Depression and I really did not know how to deal with it. This I believe was the beginning of many years of Depression and Anxiety.

During treatment, I was able to tell James how I felt, why I chose the behaviors I did and I was able to work on things in my past that I needed to. The hospital suggested a half way house after the 30 days of treatment and I agreed, although I was very hesitant. During this time, my mom took Brianna to the restaurant with her daily, she was a joy to have there and the senior citizens just loved it when she would as if they wanted "moking" or "no moking." James continued to work and he came to the cities to visit me on the weekend of our anniversary. We ended up staying at a nice hotel and having a nice weekend together.

I left the half way house early, partly because I did not feel like I fit in and partly because I was so lonesome for my family. James and I began counseling with a Christian counselor and our marriage was the best it had ever been. He was no long belittling me and we really respected each other. We attended church every week and met some super nice people. They were also our neighbors so to speak because in the country your neighbors are not super close.

JAYDEN

James and I decided we wanted another baby and about a year later we found out we were going to be parents again! I had a very good pregnancy and the C-section was planned this time so I did not have the same trauma as I had with Brianna's birth. Brianna went to "big sister" school to learn how to be a big sister. The kids brought a doll so they could practice being a big sister. Brianna was so proud of herself when she graduated "big sister school." We went to the hospital on October 29th, 1987; while waiting for the surgery to start, James was gazing out the hospital window that overlooks the Mississippi river and he said "It would be a great day for goose hunting"! I could not believe it, but that was James, he could fit right in with the Duck Dynasty men, but that is whom I married. Jayden came in the world at 1:30p.m. on October 29, 1987. Jayden weighed 7lbs. 8oz and was a wonderful baby, he was a good eater and I was able to breast-feed him, unlike Brianna whom I had difficulty with and had to bottle-feed. Things were going well and when I got home my grandma came and stayed to help after surgery because I could not do a lot of the things required of a toddler and baby. During my first evening, while eating supper I got a phone call from my dad. He was living in Minneapolis at the time and because of his drinking problem he did not have a place to live. He called me to see if I could take him in! He told me that if I did not, he would have to sleep on a park bench in Minneapolis! I told him that I could not and that I just had a baby. Once again, I felt guilty, but what parent puts that kind of burden on a child. My grandma took the phone and told him not to call here anymore that it was not the responsibility of his kids to take care of him. I knew that with our financial circumstances we could not take care of another person. I wondered what he would do without help.

Life went on and I went back to work. One day as I came home from work and Jayden was seven months old; I had the girl that lived next-door baby sit for me. When I came in the house, I rounded the corner to see Jayden projectile vomit across the living room and then go into a seizure, he was just 7 months old. I was terrified and told Jenny that we needed to take him to the hospital. I drove and Jenny held Jayden. When we got to the hospital his lips were blue and he was still seizing and gasping for breath, and I was in a panic. The nurses grabbed him from me and proceeded to take in into the emergency room cubicle, the Doctor gave him a shot of Phenobarbital and waited a few minutes, nothing was happening, he was still seizing and they called the helicopter from the Children's Hospital in the Twin Cities, and while we waited for the helicopter, they gave him another shot. Finally, he quit seizing and the Doctor told me that he gave him enough Phenobarbital to put down a horse. Jaydens's seizure lasted 45 minutes, this was unheard of for a febrile seizure. He spent the week in the hospital and 6 months on a daily course of Phenobarbital. This was just the beginning for my poor baby. We had a first birthday party for Jayden and I made him a baseball cake. He could not drink cows' milk so I made a baseball separately on the cake that was made with his formula. He was a very happy baby and had the biggest grin.

Jayden and James had a very special bond; he would "help" his dad work on his car because James was rebuilding a Ford

Pinto while Jayden was in his walker. I worked opposite shifts of James so that we did not have to pay daycare, I was usually home before James had to be to work. Brianna was thrilled to have a little brother and was such a good big sister. Everything was going great the fall and winter of 1988. Our little family was complete and we were a very happy family. That winter we had Brianna and Jayden dedicated at the Evangelical Free church that we were attending.

THE ACCIDENT

The spring of 1989 was a warm one and on Good Friday, March 24, 1989 James did not have to be to work until 3:00p.m. so my sister, Brianna and I went shopping for my sister's wedding which was to be in the fall of the year. My brother-in-law Brian was staying at our house for a few months until he finished his vocational degree so he was going to go fishing in the afternoon while we were shopping in St. Cloud. We usually got Theresa to baby-sit because she was a friend of the family and we went to the same church. I also went to bible study with her parents. So, James went about 1:30p.m. to pick up Theresa at her house about 3 miles away and bring her back to watch Jayden. Brian stayed home and watched Jayden so James did not have to get him in a car seat for such a short trip. Jayden sat in his high chair and ate cheerios while Brian waited for James and gave him cheerios in his high chair while he was waiting.

Brian was waiting and about 1:00pm he heard a horrible squeal; they say you could hear it all the way to the grade school a mile and a half away. Brian ran out to see what happened and saw a sight he would never get over. There on the tracks was James' crumpled International Scout and the train had hit it and he could see his brother who was killed on impact. He ran in to call 911. He also called his parents and my mom. They all came over to the house including Theresa's parents. James and Theresa were killed instantly. I was told that while we were shopping, they called the mall in St. Cloud to have us paged because they did not know where we were and we did not have cell phones at that time. On the way home the radio was playing and we shut it off so we could talk about the wedding. I understand that the accident was put on the radio before it was released from the sheriff's department. I am so thankful we did not hear about it on the way home. The St. Cloud Times had a front-page picture of the accident, which showed the mangled truck and a baby's red snowsuit on the tracks. It was quite a dramatic picture being black and white with a red snow suit on the tracks. I did not see it until the following day.

I got home about 2:30 p.m. and the train tracks were clear so I drove up my driveway as usual. I could not comprehend the fact that there were 6-8 cars in the driveway and that my brother was coming out to take Brianna for a drive. I went into the front door and all these people were sitting in my kitchen and looking somber. I looked around and asked, "Sure, I leave and you guys have a party without me"! I guess it never dawned on me that something horrible could have happened. Then my mom stepped up to me and told me that, my husband's truck had been hit by a train. The first thing that came to my mind was to go to the hospital so I could see him. Unfortunately, that was not possible because he was killed instantly she said. I could not even comprehend this news. I leaned up against the door and slumped to the ground in pure agony. I just sat there sobbing and I did not know what to do, I then started feeling like I was going to be sick and I had to get away from everyone, so I ran straight to the bathroom and locked the door. In the bathroom I sobbed and sobbed until my body was sore and I was exhausted, after about 20 minutes, I got it together and went back out into the kitchen. I was then told that James was not the only one in the truck that Theresa was also with him because he was bringing her back to baby-sit. My mom then told me Theresa was killed too. I do not know how I even went on after hearing this; I was so hysterical because I felt responsible for her death. If I had not been shopping James would not have needed a sitter and they both would be alive today. My memory is kind of foggy after that, I do remember them bringing my little girl in and I had to tell her that her daddy went to heaven and that we would not be able to see him again on this earth. She was five years old, who must deal with death at the age of five? I felt so helpless; I could not fix it for my little girl and my baby. My little Jayden would never know his daddy, he was only eighteen months old and there was nothing I could do to help. My little girl would have to grow up without a daddy just like I did, that is something I swore would never happen to her, that choice was taken away from me. Where was God when he was coming home, how could he let this happen to two people who loved him so? It is a question that haunted my thoughts for a very long time. I was very angry with God because I felt that he could have prevented this horrible accident.

The next days were a blur, I had to decide for James' funeral and burial, my in-laws wanted to take care of the burial and headstone and wanted him to be buried in Willmar, which was fine with me, that was his hometown, he grew up there. We had to go and pick out a casket. Who must do this at the age of twenty-four? I did not know anyone who had lost someone so young.... We got the arrangements made and went to Sunday service; it was Easter Sunday. The songs that they play in church for Easter are very hard to hear when you have just lost your best friend and husband. The visitation was held at Dingman's Funeral Home in Annandale. The family had a private visitation first then the others could come and pay their respects. We walked up to the casket, my little girl and me and they had put out yellow flowers in pots about 3 feet away from the casket so that we could not look any closer. He looked so young, he had the beard he loved and he had no glasses but I guess he did not need them, he should not be in there, he should be holding his kids, smiling and being alive! But he was not and even at the age of five Brianna was so intuitive. She looked at James and said that she did not think that was her daddy, I asked her why?

She responded, because he did not have on his glasses (James always wore glasses). The funeral director took her little hand and took her back to a room where he had a box of glasses and she picked out the ones that looked like her daddy's and together they put them on James. Then she was satisfied and said; "now he looks like my daddy." My heart ached for my little girl and boy.

There were so many people that came through, some have said around 400. I cannot remember even one. It was such a blur to me. My doctor had put me on medication because they were worried about my mental health. I now wonder if that was a good idea. His funeral was beautiful, lots of lilies and a nice sermon. I spent most of it with my head in my lap sobbing, wishing it were all a dream. After the funeral we had to drive to Willmar for the burial and then back to the church for a lunch. I cannot remember much. After James' funeral we had to start all over and go to Theresa's funeral and visitation. The days were just exhausting. I remember during the days after while I stayed at my mom's house, strangers were calling with offerings of help but I could not cope with much at the time. I wish they would have called a couple of weeks after because that is when you really need people, after everyone goes home.

After the funeral and everything, I think I just lost it. I went out with Theresa's brother the week after the funeral, I was terrified of being alone; I went from my mom's house to living with James and had never lived alone. I started drinking and partying and went out with several men that were not good for me. Once again, I associated sex with love. I felt that I was loved if I slept with a guy. I am sure this comes from being sexually abused as a child. I did not care I just wanted to be numb and these are the guys that could help me be numb. They did not care about me and I did not care about them it was just someone to party with and forget all the problems in my life. I was not heavy at all, but I lost so much weight that I was down to about 118 lbs., which was less than I weighed in high school. I think the trauma and stress just weighed on me and I could not eat.

Many people tried to help me and would say things to me about my behavior, but at the time I just did not care. After about 6 months a realization came to me that my kids needed me and I got back on the right path of being a responsible adult and a mother to my children. I think knowing God as a little girl really helped me because I knew what I was doing was wrong and I had sworn I would not be a bad mother to my children. After all, they only had me. After the accident, I contacted a lawyer. I was not sure if I had a case or not but I had heard that the train did not blow their horn at the crossing which was required. Most of the time I was not too involved with the case except to prepare for trial. I probably should have had a different lawyer; I think things would have turned out differently. The railroad tried to say that something was going on between James and Theresa and I knew better. My attorney said we should settle and I did not know any better. They said that it would be the best thing to do, so we settled out of court. Money was put away for when Brianna and Jayden turned eighteen. It was not a lot but it was something.

NEW HOUSE-NEW BEGINNINGS

I tried college and I could not concentrate, so I just decided to be a mom and not worry about anything else. In the fall of 1989, I ended up buying a house next door to the house that I had owned with James so that the kids did not have to move but I had a newer house with less upkeep. Things were finally starting to get better; I had decided I was not going to date anymore because I just believed that if it were right, God would send me someone. In the spring of 1990, I got my tax statement in the mail that said my house was worth $75,000. Well, I had just paid $65,000 for it so I thought I could go and protest and get my market value reduced on my tax statement, which would then reduce the amount of taxes I had to pay. So, I had to go to the town hall when they had their board of review and talk to the Sherburne County Assessors. As I was waiting for my turn, I had Jayden with me and he was into his terrible two's. He could not sit for five minutes and I was constantly picking him up off the floor and trying to make him behave. Finally, it was my turn to go up to talk with the board. I told them about the $10,000 difference in what I paid and what they said it was worth and they said they would send someone out to reappraise the house.

A couple of days later Brad came out from the assessor's office and I showed him around the house, out to the garage and down to the barn. I had horses at the time and my horse Princess I had gotten back did not like men. The next thing I know she was charging towards Brad and I had to step behind him and grab her and put her up. I was so embarrassed but all was o.k. Brad told me he would call me in a couple of days and let me know what their decision was.

The next day I got a phone call from the assessor's office, it was about 5:30 p.m. so it was after hours, it was Brad and he said he had my assessment done and they were going to lower it to $65,000. He then proceeded to ask me if I would like to go out to dinner with him. I was nervous because I did not know him, but I thought about it and finally said I would. So, we made plans for Saturday night.

Brad came and picked me up and we went to a nice dinner and was able to talk and visit like old friends. I really liked him, but wanted to take it slow because of my past. He dropped me off at home and I know he wanted to kiss me but I felt like I did not know him well enough so I just said thank you for the dinner and went into the house. He gave me his phone number so if I wanted, I could call him.

I called him a couple of days later and invited him to my sister's house (she had bought the house that James and I lived in next door to me). Everyone liked him and I liked him even more after my family met him so we started dating. He brought a bag of Jelly Beans for my kids, Brianna proceeded to tell him she did not like Jelly Beans and Jayden said "I do!" I met his parents shortly after and met Danny his son. Danny and Jayden were only fifteen months apart so they got along great. Brad's parents were wonderful and I felt right at home with them. Brad and I dated for a couple of months and since he was living with his parents after his divorce, I asked him if he wanted to move in with us. Probably not the best move on my part, but that is how it worked-out.

Brad was great with the kids and things were going along smoothly, Brianna and I started showing horses and the boys would spend time fishing, hanging out and riding bikes, Jayden's favorite thing to do. When Jayden was two, we heard banging in his room, Brad ran in to check on him and he was having another febrile seizure. We ran him back up the emergency room and his seizure again lasted twenty minutes. He spent a couple of days in the hospital and then back home. Jayden tended to be a very active boy (that is putting it mildly); he was always getting hurt, needing stitches among other things. It got to the point where we were afraid to take him to emergency room, thinking that they would think we were abusing him! One day him and Brianna were playing in the basement when they came up and Brianna said Jayden hit his head on the cement. I took him to emergency once again and they did all the tests, including x-ray and CT scan. The doctor said that he looked fine and I could take him home. As we were heading out the door a nurse came running out and said that they made a mistake and

Jayden had a skull fracture and a concussion and did I want to keep him here over night. Of course I did, we lived to far from the hospital not to stay and have them watch him. This was just the beginning for Jayden. He struggled growing up with attention deficit disorder. I attribute this to the severe seizures he had as a baby and lack of oxygen. Little did we know that there would be many more consequences of those seizures. Jayden tended to have a very low frustration level. He could not handle it if you said no or tried to get him to play with something else. To say that he was difficult would be putting it mildly. My mother thought I had the patience of a saint dealing with him. My thoughts were that he had enough to deal with in his little life that I just had to be patient with him. But, believe me I could get frustrated too, who would not!

MARRIED

Brad and I were married on July 4th 1992 in a small ceremony on our front lawn. Brianna and the boys participated in the wedding, she was eight and the boys were four and three. We had a pig roast after for our reception. Brad and I never discussed children, but I wanted another with him. The kids were in school and they had their hobbies. Brianna loved her horses and was in 4-H and Jayden and Danny loved riding bikes and would go to the BMX track in St. Cloud. Life goes on and before you know it 10 years had passed with the ups and downs of raising children, putting two families together and all the pitfalls of a blended family. I really felt we did well considering second marriages are even more likely to end in divorce if you believe the statistics.

In 1992 Brad got side work drawing plats for a title company in St. Cloud, eventually I began doing them and then began working for the title company as an abstract typist. I worked for them for nine months, and then got laid off after Christmas of 1993. This opened an opportunity to do abstracting on a contract basis, so I started an abstracting company. I ran this company for fifteen years with quite a bit of success until the bottom dropped out of the economy.

Brianna and I were showing horses quite heavily and I was always nervous pulling a trailer, but when I started having heart problems, it put a whole new light on driving a truck and trailer. I had problems with a racing heart (tachycardia) several times and it got to the point where I did not feel comfortable driving because I would get so dizzy. We had great friends that would haul the horses for us to different events including the County Fair. I tried to find a doctor that could help me with my heart issues. I went to the Mayo Clinic in Rochester and they put me on a medication but it did not help. I went to the University of Minnesota and got the same results. I ended up in the St. Cloud Hospital on the telemetry ward where they monitor heart patients. I was in my twenties and very frustrated. My heart would speed up in the daytime and at night when I slept it would drop below 40 which set off all kinds of alarms. After five years

I finally found a doctor that could help me at Mercy Heart Center in Coon Rapids. Dr. Redde gave me a Holter heart monitor to wear and we finally got some answers. The summer of 1999 I had the worst attack I would have; it was hot at the fair 110 degrees with the heat index, Brianna was showing and we had to strip the horses saddles off when she was done with a class and sponge them down and by the next class, they were dry and we would have to saddle them back up. Brianna was still young so a lot of it depended on me. It did not take long and my heart started pounding, I could feel it in my throat. I had a Holter monitor on at the time to track my heart. I went to my mom's where we stayed during fair and called my doctor. He said my heart was beating at 210 beats per minute and I needed medication, so he called in the medication to Target in Buffalo, but driving was a problem and no one was home to drive me. I decided I had to get the medicine so I got in the truck and told Brianna that if I pass out to hit the brakes. We did not have cell phones at the time so I was on my own. I made it to Target, but things felt worse so I had to call Brad and my brother-in-law to come and get me and drive my truck back to my mom's. I just laid in bed in the air conditioning until my heart finally calmed down, it was a total of ten hours of a racing heart. After this incident I was back in the doctor's office and he felt that I needed a pacemaker so in September of 1999 I got my first pacemaker, I was 35 years old. I still had problems with Atrial Fibrillation even with the pacemaker. The doctors did not know why my heart was acting up but said it was probably idiopathic, which means they don't know what it is.

January 2nd 2002, I found out I was pregnant. This came as a huge surprise since I had been to fertility doctors and my own ob/gyn said I probably would not get pregnant. We were thrilled when we found out. Brianna and I went looking at colleges the prior spring, we drove to Ohio and looked at Findley University and Carthage College and River Falls Wisconsin. She was thrilled with the colleges but decided that she just did not want to miss the new baby coming so she decided to go to St. Cloud State University instead. Brianna was set to graduate high school in June 2002 and I was 6 months pregnant! We were able to have a nice party for her before the doctor told me I needed to take it easy because of my heart and because I had developed gestational diabetes. I was so grateful because Brianna had gone with me so much, she knew how to do my work so she took over once I had to be off my feet and after I had the baby.

Manny was born on August 23, 2002 he weighed 7lbs 2oz and was a perfect baby. The kids and Brad were so thrilled with little Manny. Brianna was 18, Jayden was 15 and Danny was 14 when Manny was born. I had always had trouble with depression, anxiety, and post-partum depression, but I never had the anxiety problems after the kids were born. After Danny was born, I had such anxiety it brought me to the emergency room twice until the doctor figured out it was post-partum anxiety and put me on a medication. After I was put on medication things were again calm and I only had problems occasionally.

Brianna worked for me doing abstracting while she was in college so I could stay home with Manny after about six months I decided I wanted to go back to work. I found a great day care for Manny and I went back to work. Manny was always getting colds and runny noses and I could not understand why he was always sick. Because we have allergies in the family, I decided to take him to an allergist. We had been bringing him with to the horse shows, letting him ride lead line and he loved it. We found out from the allergist that Manny is allergic to horses! This seemed like to worst news to hear because we loved our horses and I had just gotten my dream horse a Paint horse that we called Glory; she was a wonderful show horse with a wonderful disposition. But of course, your children come first, so I decided it was time to get out of horses. In 2006, I put everything up for sale. Sold my horses, my trailer and all my equipment and traded in my truck for an SUV. Little did I know this would be the perfect time to sell everything because soon the real estate bubble would burst and I would have no work. Soon after I was to find out I had developed Cardiomyopathy and my heart was weakening. I was managed on medication for the time being. I was scared because I had children that were all home yet. But God was watching over me and my doctor was able to catch it right away.

The spring of 2008 I came down with a stomach bug, I always got respiratory infections, but rarely got stomach bugs. I became ill on Saturday and by the end of the next week I was sick! I went to the doctor and they sent me to get fluids and then back home, hoping that would take care of the problem and I would be on the mend. I woke up Sunday morning feeling worse. My neck and back hurt, I was still running a fever so I decided I needed to go to the emergency room. Once at the hospital my knee started swelling and I was in so much pain that they had to give me Morphine for the pain. They did not know what was going on so they decided to keep me. I was in the hospital for better part of the week and they discovered I had a stomach infection and reactive arthritis from the infection. The Rheumatologist came and took fluid off my knee. Finally, by the end of the week I could go home to recover. According to the doctor only 1% of people ever get reactive arthritis and most of them are men. It seems I always end up with weird disorders that nobody normal ever gets!

MY GROWN-UP KIDS

The spring of 2006 Jayden graduated from Kimball High School and enlisted in the Marine Corps. He left for boot camp three days after graduation. I cried the whole way home after dropping him off. I had never had any of my kids gone like Jayden was, it would be a long five years while he was in the military. He was so excited to go, we had to be happy for him. We were so proud of Jayden and promised him we would have his party when he came home from boot camp in the fall. Jayden graduated September 9, 2006 from MCRD San Diego and we all went to California to watch him graduate. While we were in San Diego, we drove to Santee to see my old house. I could not believe how much things had changed. Everything seemed smaller and there were a lot more houses packed into the open spaces that I remember. When we got home, we rented the town hall and had a party to celebrate his high school graduation and his graduation from the Marine Corps. I could not believe my son was a private in the marines! Jayden was home for two weeks, but we did not see much of him. He came in the door went to his room, proceeded to dump his duffel bag in the middle of his room and said see ya! I guess at that age your friends are more important than boring old parents.

Jayden went back to the marines and went to school in Maryland for Combat Videography. We were very proud of him. He then got stationed at Quantico, Virginia where he was stationed from 2007-2011. Jayden worked mostly with QTV on base and did videos for the Marine Corps of things like retirements of Generals, the Marine Corps birthday ball, and promotions, etc. He also had a video in Iron Man II that he sent to Hollywood for a part in the movie, it was so much fun to be able to tell people to watch the movie and look for the part he had submitted. He loved his job and planned on the marines for his career. I recall going to church and asking for prayers for my son. I was lost without him. He would call me every day and when I would pick up, he would say "hello Mother dear, how are you"? I so looked forward to those calls.

Jayden called me on evening and said he woke up in the morning and there was blood on his pillow. I thought that maybe he had bit his cheek grinding his teeth; because I knew he had ground his teeth when he was young. I told him to try a mouth guard. This happened a couple of more times and we were all puzzled. Jayden had a job to do for the marines off base and he went with several other photographers and videographers in a van to Tattoo, which is a battle of the bands including bands from all over the world as well as the Marine Corps Band. After they got done shooting video, they were going to go get something to eat, as it was late, around midnight. Jayden was tired and began dozing off when he went into a Grand Mal Seizure. His fellow marines pulled him out onto the sidewalk and called 911, a nurse from inside the bar that they were in front of came out and helped them get Jayden positioned right so he would not hurt himself. His seizure lasted 5-7 minutes. This was a long seizure. An ambulance was called and he was taken to the local hospital and checked out since as far as anyone knew this was his first seizure. Of course, we did not know he had been having seizures as he slept and that was what was causing the blood on his pillow. Jayden kept this from me for a while and only talked to his sister because he was afraid of my reaction.

Jayden was then sent to Walter Reed Army Medical Hospital, a hospital for servicemen for further testing, in Bethesda Maryland. He had an EEG and an MRI. The EEG came back normal, but the MRI showed scarring on his left temporal lobe, which indicates epilepsy. This would be the end of Jayden's career in the Marines. Jayden stayed in the Marine Corps for two more years while he was working on getting disability. In the military they decide if you are disabled and like everything in the military it takes a long time. The first offer from the military was 10% disabled. He called me and asked me what I thought. I told him that 10% was for a hang nail, not a brain disorder. I suggested he get an attorney on base. He consulted an attorney and resubmitted his paperwork for disability and they came back with 40% I believe. He had to get a certain percentage which I believe is 40% to be medically retired and get his health insurance for the rest of his life. This was so important because he was going to need ongoing care. He was medically retired on November 9, 2011.

Brianna decided college just was not for her and she decided to try something else for a while. She took a job at Becker Furniture World where she met her Phillip. Brianna and Phillip dated for a couple of years and on Thanksgiving of 2008, Phil proposed to Brianna. We were thrilled, Phillip was a great guy and came from a wonderful home. Brianna was so happy! She was so excited because he grew up out in the country like she did. They were married on October 17, 2009 and they bought their first house. Brianna then switched jobs to work for a national bank in St. Cloud where she is a business analyst, she has had several promotions and is the head of the credit department for a national bank. We were blessed with our first Grandchild on March 23, 2011 a beautiful baby boy named James, after his grandpa James. We could not be prouder of that little boy. Jayden and Danny were thrilled to be uncles.

Grandma missed the birth of her great great grandson, but she knew he was coming. She went into hospice care and about a week later September 29, 2010 she went to heaven to be with her Lord. It was a sad day for all of us, but we were happy she was free of the sufferings of her health. Grandma was an integral part of me growing up; she introduced me to Sunday school and Jesus, and spent a lot of time with me growing up. I still miss her, but she gave me her Bible upon her death and when I get lonesome, I go to her Bible and read, it is nice to be able to read what was important to her and what she highlighted to be helpful to her.

Brad and I have enjoyed 20 years together, Manny is in 5th grade and we are looking forward to spending a lot of time with our Grandson. I am currently waiting to see if I can qualify for disability, since working has become quite difficult for me. But in the meantime, I am enjoying my family and thanking God for the blessings that have come my way and the lessons I have learned from my past. I t was around this time that I was exhausted all the time and did not know what was wrong with me. I went to the cardiologist and was diagnosed with heart failure. My ejection fraction was about 25 and that is the amount of blood that is being pumped out of my heart. It should be around 55. I was put on more medication for the heart failure and eventually it went up to about 45-50 and stayed there for quite a while. I was doing o.k. I took a job with AmeriCorps tutoring math of all things. I thought I was terrible at math but maybe that helped because the kids I tutored had trouble and I could understand what they were going through. I loved tutoring and the year I spent at Clearview was a great year. According the AmeriCorps when I started you could only tutor one year but unfortunately, they had trouble getting people to join so they changed the program to 2 years. I rejoined because it was so close to home and I felt like I was making a real difference in these kids' lives. During the second year of tutoring, I was told I had to tutor in the library. This was o.k., it was generally quiet but I kept getting sick. I developed pneumonia and could not shake it. During Christmas break I was getting better but then as soon as I was back to school it came back. I finally told the principal that I had to quit because of my health. During this time, I had applied for disability because of my heart and my other health problems. I thought there was something in the library that was making me sick since I was not sick the year before. The school had someone out to do some testing and found out that the mold in the carpet was high, so high that they had to have the whole library torn up and tile put in and the books cleaned up. The school was happy because they got a new library.

My sister-in-law was helping me with my disability claim. I was denied twice and was feeling very frustrated. I could not work because I was sick but struggled to get disability. After the two denials I was told, I would have to go to court and it would go before a judge. My sister-in-law flew here from Kentucky for the hearing but had forgotten to send in one piece of paper so she brought it with to give the judge. The judge told us she would not hear our case because of that one piece of paper. We were so disgusted because Tanya had to fly here from Kentucky and we drove to the Twin Cities for the hearing. All we could do is go home. The hearing was rescheduled for June. When we went back, we sat before a judge and a doctor that she had hired to read my medical charts. The hearing lasted about 5 minutes and he said there is no way that I could work. He said I would probably miss at least 2 days of work a week and she approved it.

2012

2012 began quietly, Manny and I decided to get into showing rabbits, which was a great hobby for us. We raised Mini Rex rabbits. Kristy, my niece, also attends shows and I feel good about being able to mentor them with the rabbits as well as dogs. They belong in 4-H and are enjoying it like I did growing up. In January I was diagnosed with eosinophilic esophagitis along with gastrointestinal reflux. I took medication for that and it helped quite a bit. I would have trouble eating and swallowing and would choke and cough quite a bit. Later, the end of June on a Friday I had a stomachache that would not go away, I assumed it was nothing so I did not call the doctor. That night things had gotten worse and I started running a fever. I told Brad that I probably should go to the hospital. Manny had a friend overnight and they were sleeping, so Brad went and woke them up and we headed to the hospital. We were planning on going to Kentucky to visit family the following Friday for the 4th of July which happens to be our anniversary. The doctors in the emergency room decided with the help of an ultra sound that I was having a gall bladder attack and that I would need surgery. I was not too concerned because gall bladder surgery is a one-day surgery and I would be home by the following day. The surgery was scheduled for the next day since they did not feel it was an emergency. I spent the night in pain and on pain medication and when noon the next day came around, I was taken down to the operating room for my surgery. My family said goodbye and I was whisked away. The next thing I remember was being told that my blood pressure had dropped considerably and they did not know what was going on except that I needed to go to the Intensive Care Unit. I spent 36 hours in intensive care, my Kidneys were shutting down and I was going into respiratory failure. The doctors decided I was going Septic. I do not remember a lot about those days in the hospital, but I do remember having horrible hallucinations of spiders on my bed and on the walls. I would tell myself that they were not real and close my eyes. Brianna and Jayden would come and visit along with Brad and Manny. Brianna commented that she was walking down the hall one day and she could hear me breathing all the way down the hall. She asked the nurses what was going on and they said oh that is your mom. She was very upset and asked what they were doing about it. It was discussed between my family members about moving me to a hospital in the twin cities when a hospitalist came and looked at everything and put me on a strong antibiotic. There is nothing worse than feeling helpless in bed and not being able to get yourself up for the bathroom or to do minor self-care. I had a lot of family come visit, including my sister whom I did not recognize at first. The one thing I felt was a sense of peace, I felt like I was probably dying but I was not afraid. I knew God was with me and I could feel his presence. While I was in the hospital pastor Tony came to visit me and prayed with me, I truly felt close to God and felt him with me during this trying time. I had always been afraid of death with all the people I have had close to me die, but after this experience in the hospital, I have a new peaceful feeling about death. In one way I kind of wished I would have died, but then I think of my kids who only have one parent left and I know that it would be a traumatic event for them to endure and I do not want anyone to have to endure what I have in my life.

My husband's sister and dad came to Minnesota when I was coming home from the hospital, Tanya was a registered nurse so it would be helpful having her here. I came home maybe a bit early but I was tired of the hospital after nearly two weeks. My mom came up and brought me a hospital bed that they set up in our family room so I could be in bed but still watch TV and visit with people. It helped being able to adjust the head of the bed like in the hospital. I slowly recovered and we went back to church. We had been going to the Alliance church in Clearwater and we really liked it. We took classes and became members. We loved the pastor he was a great speaker and very relatable. My niece and nephew also liked the church and went to youth group, they got Manny going to youth group as well and they all had a great time.

Jayden was well maintained on his medication and had gone a full 16 months without a seizure when he had a breakthrough seizure. I happened to be on the phone with him when he went into this seizure. He was not making any sense and I could hear banging. I got really scared and called Brianna. Brianna worked in St. Cloud where Jayden was living so I asked her to go and check on him. I was watching my grandson at the time so it took me a bit to get ready to go to St. Cloud. Brianna called and said he had a seizure and she was taking him to the hospital and he was walking around in a daze looking for his wallet. This is typical of a seizure that the person would be disoriented after the seizure. He went to the Emergency Room and I met them there. The doctor checked him out and he was okay, he just needed to go home and rest. The breakthrough seizure is generally an issue with their medication. I felt Jayden needed an increase in his medication. He had gained weight so I thought maybe he needed an increase in his medication. So, Jayden made an appointment with the local VA. Jayden did not drive because he was worried, he could have a seizure and hit someone with his car. I usually went in a took him where he needed to go, otherwise he took the bus or rode his bike. When we got the VA, they proceeded to tell us that his doctor did not show up and we would have to reschedule. So, we rescheduled to about 10 days later. This was about October 10, 2012 when the rescheduled appointment was.   I also took him to this appointment and they said they could not do anything and that he would have to make an appointment with Neurology at the Minneapolis Veterans Administration. When they sent him the letter his appointment was not for 70 days. I believe this was December 21st. Since we did not know that much about epilepsy and had never heard of SUDEP (Sudden Unexpected Death in Epilepsy) we were not concerned about his wait. We found out later that if Jayden had a seizure because his were Tonic Clonic seizures he was to be seen immediately, this was noted on his file at the VA. So, life went on and Jayden was putting a lot into college and having a good time with his friends and his brother Danny. They loved riding their bikes and doing BMX tricks. It was one of his hobbies that he had loved since he was a young kid. We all went to my Moms for Thanksgiving November 22, 2012, my uncle was there and took family pictures. It was a wonderful day, we all had so much fun. Brianna's family was there so we had James and he was just a baby. Jayden and James had a very special bond. Jayden was so happy that he could be in Minnesota when his nephew was a baby. Monday November 26, 2012 Jayden went to be with the Lord.

Manny was 10 years old and we were into 4-H with the rabbits and the dog project. We had a golden retriever named Jo that he was working with, she was old and he wanted a new dog. His pick was a German Shepherd puppy so we went and found him a puppy. As this puppy was growing up, she developed terrible allergies that we were not really equipped to handle but we did the best we could. On November 26th we were having a 4-H meeting at our house as we all took turns hosting the meetings. Right in the middle of the meeting there was a knock on the door. I answered it and it was a Sherburne County Sheriff at the door. I was not surprised since we live on the highway and we have had them stop before looking for people that maybe broke down on the highway. The Sheriff asked if he could speak to us and my husband came down as well. I said sure and we went into the family room down stairs where it was more private. I guess I should have known something was wrong after James' accident, you would think I would learn. When we got down to the basement family room the Sheriff proceeded to tell us that they found Jayden and he had died. I immediately dropped to the ground in shock. I sobbed and sobbed. There was no way my 25-year-old son could be gone! I wanted to go see him. I wanted to hold him. I could not even comprehend this news. How could it happen to me twice in a lifetime that someone so close to me has died again! I felt like the wind was knocked out of me and that I could not go on with my life anymore. I asked them what happened and they told me he was studying at his desk and his roommates came home and found him lying face first in his computer. They took him down to the ground and started CPR and called the ambulance. The rescue workers worked on him for 45 minutes and could not bring him back. I was just sick; how could a perfectly healthy 25-year-old guy die from no apparent reason? They told me I could not see him and that they had taken him to the Ramsey County Coroner. The Ramsey County Coroner is where they take people when they do not know how or why they died or if it is a suspected murder or something. Since they could see no reason for his death he went there. My daughter Brianna was at our house for the 4-H meeting and I was so thankful, I did not have to call her and tell her, her brother died. I called my mom and her and my step dad came right away as well as my sister and brother. The chaplain from the Sherburne County Sheriff's office came and was there for us, he prayed for us and Jayden and gave us the support we needed hearing this horrible news.

The kids and the other parents went next door and cancelled the meeting. Manny went with them as well and came back later when we were not in such shock and could explain to him that his brother had passed away and was with God now. Brianna spent the night and we just sat up all night not knowing what to do. I could not sleep anyway and just waited for the coroner to call, we made a pot of coffee and sat up talking, remembering my precious boy. While we were waiting, we started looking on google to see what could have happened with him. The coroner called around midnight and asked a bunch of questions. I told him that he had epilepsy and while we were googling, we ran across something called SUDEP, this acronym stands for Sudden Unexpected Death in Epilepsy. I asked the coroner if this could be what he died from and he said of course but that they had to do the autopsy and check toxicology and then he would have a better answer. I think it was the longest night of my life. I do not know what I would have done without Brianna here. The next day we had to start making funeral arrangements. I did not want to be put on any medicine for the stress because I wanted to remember everything. Not like when James died and I was really drugged to get me through it. All I could think of is that Jayden is in heaven with James and, he could see his daddy again. His funeral was so beautiful. He had several Marine Corps buddies that came and they were able to do a small ceremony during the funeral and they placed their pins in with Jayden. I am sure they were devastated because they were all so young and Jayden was so important to them. The funeral was quite extended because we had the visitation on Friday night at the funeral home, the funeral on Saturday at the church with Pastor Tony presiding then we had to wait until Monday for the burial. Since he was being buried in a veteran's cemetery, they only do burials during the week. It was December so it was quite cold, they had the burial service in a rotunda indoors, the 21-gun salute was just outside the building.

It was horrible to leave him there. Although now, I feel him more here at home than in the cemetery.

As the day's past after the funeral, I felt him getting further away from me. I do not really know how to explain it. I just know that I was in such a state that I felt like he was getting further away from me. I do not remember much about that year. After the funeral we felt Manny really needed something. He was so lost without his brother. His German Shepherd was not working out because of all the extra care she needed and I was in no shape to take care of her. I had a friend that said she could take her; she had a ranch in Montana and she made all her own dog food so she could put her on a specialized diet. She also knew a lady who had Mini Australian Shepherd puppies and she only had one left so I sent her the money and she drove back to Minnesota to drop off the puppy and pick up the German Shepherd. The night we went to pick up the puppy it was New Years Eve and it was -20°F and we had to drive over an hour to Alexandria to pick him up. It was all worth it when we saw Manny grin and hold the little fur ball. Manny named him Zeus because he was into the Percy Jackson books. Zeus was 8 weeks old, a Black Tri with Blue eyes. He was striking. I thought it would really help Manny to have something of his own since he was basically an only child since his siblings were either grown or gone.

AFTER JAYDEN'S DEATH

My life is split in two, before Jayden died and after Jayden died. After he died, I did some writing, I wrote a couple of poems that were published by Minnesota Epilepsy Foundation, I was trying to find something to help make me feel better. I decided that I needed to go to grief counseling. I felt I did not know how to grieve. What is the right or wrong way to grieve. I know when James died, I did not handle it well at all and it was not in my best interest to fall of the cliff again with Jayden's death. I was afraid of how I would react since I have not dealt with loss very well in my past. I went to a grief counselor in St. Cloud. I was able to tell her how I felt and I did not have to worry about making someone else feel bad. That was my fear that if I talked to family and I broke down crying that it would make them feel bad. I did that after James died, I did not talk about him because I would tear up. It was not the right way to deal with it when your kids ask why you never talk about him. I tried to explain to them that I did not want to upset them by talking about him and me getting upset. So, it was such a relief to be able to talk about Jayden, talk about missing him and feeling like my heart was torn out of my chest. I talked about what we were going to miss. He would never get married, never have children, or finish college. So many things I would miss. I would miss his daily calls, seeing him at family functions, driving him to appointments for his epilepsy. I questioned why we did not push to get him into the neurologist sooner. Losing an adult child is so difficult because you have no control. I could not take over and make his appointments, I could not advocate for him, except after his death. I kept going to counseling for about six months and felt I could continue without counseling. At the one-year anniversary of Jayden's death I wanted to do something special to mark this date. I talked to Brianna and some of Jayden's friends that still worked at Quantico in the Video/Photography building. We decided as a group that we wanted to do a PSA. Brianna and I flew to Quantico and went to the Marine Corps Base where we got together with his friends and filmed the PSA. We put it on YouTube as well as sent copies to all the state epilepsy foundations in the United States. We got a lot of feedback because people were just starting to talk about SUDEP and this brought SUDEP to the forefront of peoples thinking. I was gung-ho to get information about SUDEP out and what people can do to take care of themselves and do everything they can to prevent SUDEP. I was able to do some speaking in the area as well as out of state. I spoke at the Epilepsy Day at the Capitol at the Minnesota State Capitol. I also went to a few conferences, the first was in Virginia. The conference is for lay people as well as professional people that work with people with epilepsy or are researching epilepsy. I was able to meet several other families that were impacted by epilepsy and SUDEP. The conference is called PAME (Partners Against Mortality in Epilepsy), I was able to learn a lot about epilepsy over the three-day conference.

This conference is held yearly and is open to family members who have lost a person because of epilepsy. When PAME came to Minneapolis, I was able to speak and talk about Jayden and the wait we had to see a neurologist as well as what I felt had contributed to his death. I continued to advocate for Veterans and those with epilepsy. I traveled to different American Legions and VFW's trying to educate veterans on epilepsy and traumatic brain injuries that many of our veterans have had to dealt with after the current wars in the Middle East. I wanted the veterans to know how to be an advocate for themselves as well as how to do their best to prevent SUDEP. Unfortunately, I did not get a great response going to the clubs to try and educate.

In between advocating I was still a mother to a little boy and we started showing dogs. Manny started showing Zeus and he ended up finishing his championship when Manny was thirteen and he put a national champion obedience title on Zeus. Showing dogs with my son and niece was a nice break. We enjoyed it and enjoyed traveling. We went a couple of times to the Miniature American Shepherd Club Nationals in Missouri. I had made a deal with my niece that if she showed one of my girls, her name is Jazzy, and finished her championship that we would have her bred and I would keep a puppy back and she would get Jazzy. Kristy has had Jazzy for quite a while now and loves her so much. I am glad I was able to help her out. I was still so angry about the VA that more was not done to prevent Jayden from passing away. I went to see an attorney about a law suit against the VA and they were hesitant because we would be taking on the United States Government and that has not been very successful for too many people in the past. My attorney decided we would try and we started digging. This is when we found out about the flag on Jayden's record that stated, he should have an appointment right away if he had another seizure. We also found out that they said Jayden had called to reschedule his appointment the day after he had passed away. This was during the time that the VA was having problems in other states as well especially Arizona. It took quite a while but in the end the VA made us an offer to settle out of court. I had to go before the judge and I said I would settle but the only way I would settle would be if I could talk about the case. I wanted other's to be able to learn from what we went through and to advocate and insist on being seen in certain cases. Especially if they have Tonic Clonic seizures. Tonic Clonic seizures are when the seizure affects the whole body. It can be violent and after the person quits seizing, they go into what is called a post ictal state which is after the seizure. They usually are very disoriented and very tired. Eventually I did not do as much for the Epilepsy Foundation, I do not know if it was frustration because I could not do what I wanted to do with the veterans or if I just got tired. My health was a little worse, dealing with Diabetes, Heart Failure, and Cardiomyopathy. My doctor decided I needed a different pacemaker put in. The left side of my heart was not functioning like it should so I went in for another pacemaker. They added a lead to my left side and a different pacemaker called a biventricular pacemaker. It will cause the heart to be more efficient. It helped give me a little more energy.

We got another surprise in March of 2014; my granddaughter Emma was born. Grandpa was super excited because we had a little girl in our family. She has been a joy but they grow up way to fast. She is sassy and independent. James and Emma have been so good for us, I believe they truly aided in healing my heart. James is so serious and loves all sports but especially football, baseball, and basketball. He has tournaments in basketball almost every weekend during the season. Emma is in dance just like her mama and she immediately made the competition team and is very good, although I could be biased.

NEW FAMILY

The fall of 2018 I had been hearing about all these DNA testing sites. I was so desperate to know my father because not knowing left a hug hole in my heart. I thought if I knew him, I would not feel so empty and alone. So, after quite a bit of thought I sent off for two tests. Ancestry and 23 And Me to see if I could find out any close relatives. I watch a lot of crime documentaries because I wanted to be a youth probation officer. During some of these documentaries they use these DNA testing sites to find criminals. I understood how they do this because of the classes I took in college so I took the tests. It was not long before I got the tests in the mail. It is easy to do. Some tests you swab your cheek and some you spit in a small vial and send them back. I was on pins and needles waiting for these tests to come back. Pretty soon I received an email and my tests were done. There were not any close relatives on the side of my father so it involved me having to do a genealogy search so I had to start way back in the 1800's. It took me about a month of crossing people off and figuring out what children belonged to what parents, etc. I soon had it down to 6 cousins that could be my father. I decided to call and see if I could get some more information so I picked up the phone and called the first person on my list. I had to google quite a bit to find phone numbers but I was determined and I think God was at my side. I called a man in Florida and asked him if he knew anyone that could be my father. He right away said, "it's not me!" I said I was not accusing anyone and I do not want anything from anyone but information, especially health information. He calmed down and said he did a DNA test on My Heritage and I thanked him and hung up. After I got off the phone I googled "How to find your biological father?" I found out through google that I could submit my DNA that had already been sequenced to any other site to check for matches. So, the first thing I did was put it into My Heritage to see if the man I spoke with was related. To my surprise it came up that he was either an uncle, a half-brother, or a nephew. Well, that was not hard because he was nearing 80 years old so he could not be a half-brother or a nephew since he was way older than my mom. He had to be my uncle. I was so excited I could not stand it. I did it, I found my other family. I called the man back and said it showed up that he was my uncle and he said he had a fraternal twin brother and he only had one brother. I found my dad! I looked him up and unfortunately found out that he passed away from esophageal cancer. But in his obituary, it said that he had two sons so I got the names of my half-brothers! I called one of them because he had a business so it was easy to find his number. I called him a couple nights later (I had to be brave). When I got a hold of him, he was skeptical which I can totally understand. I reassured him I was not looking for anything financial, I really wanted to know them and to find out any health issues in the family. He said he was interested to but did not want to use the DNA services that I used he wanted to go through a private DNA service. We picked one and decided to each pay half of the bill. We got the swabs in the mail and did them right away and sent them back. It took a few weeks for them to return and when they did it was a match. It said we were half siblings. My family was very happy for me since this is something I have wanted since I was a teenager. I asked my brother right away if there are any health issues in the family. He told me he has Holt Oram Syndrome which is a syndrome that affects the heart and hands. I looked it up and it says that it can affect the heart either as a baby with a hole in the heart or as a young adult with the electrical system of the heart. My brother has a short thumb and it can affect arms and hands quite severely. I am lucky I do not have anything too obvious with my hands. It explained a lot about my heart problems. My doctor had never heard of it so I decided to go to the Mayo Clinic and have genetic testing done. The gene that it affects is called the TBX5 gene, it is known for cardiac and forelimb development. When I saw the genetic doctor, she did not think I had it because although my hands are small, my pinkies are crooked and my arms are on the shorter side they were not otherwise affected very much. A couple weeks later the results were back and I did carry the gene for Holt Oram Syndrome.

We decided we wanted to meet and Manny was currently looking for a college since it was the Spring before his Senior year. We decided to go to Iowa to see Iowa State University and we met both my brothers at a restaurant. We talked a lot and it was so cool to find someone I looked like! I never felt like I looked like my mom's side. This was the start of a great relationship between us. One of my brothers is a Christian and his oldest son is a Pastor in California. It was great to find this out and know that him and his wife will be someone I can talk to about my relationship with Jesus. I was fortunate enough to meet their mother as well and she was very welcoming and very sweet. The first thing she said is she always wanted a daughter. It made me feel so good to be welcomed by the family. I saw photos and could see a similarity between me and my dad when he was young.

They sent me the video of his funeral that had a lot of pictures in it. I felt like my life was much more complete now.

HEALING

In 2020 the world was hit with SARS Cov2. It was a scary time. So many deaths and people in the hospital. They were on TV constantly warning people with underlying health conditions to be careful. I truly never went anywhere, Brad went to work and he would get groceries, of course Manny was a Senior in high school so he was out and about but he understood that if someone was sick, he had to stay away from them. I was worried that it would be brought home and I would get it. After having Sepsis, I was worried. So many things were shut down. They could not have graduations indoors so schools would do outdoor graduations. Manny's school set it up like a drive-in theatre and we could hear the speaking from our phones in our cars. They had a giant screen so we could see the people speaking. Then they had a drive through where you picked up your diploma and a flower. Some of the parents put together a parade so all the graduates drove through town and people lined up on the streets and waved and congratulated the kids.

We were at a loss about a graduation party, we decided it would be outside and, in the garage, and we kept the guest list down. All went off without a hitch and nobody got sick. Thank goodness. In March of 2023 Brad got Covid. A couple days later so did I. Brad got over his quickly and I took Paxlovid because they thought it would help. After I was done with the medicine, I rebounded and got all my symptoms back and then some. I never completely got over Covid. I developed Long Covid and am dealing with many symptoms that leave me exhausted and I find it hard just to do normal everyday things. I have done a lot of thinking and decided I need to come back to Jesus. I was so angry after Jayden died that I did not really want to have anything to do with Jesus because I felt he could have prevented the deaths I have been through. I started seeing a Christian Counselor during the year of 2023-2024 and she has helped me a lot dealing with my health as well as dealing with the things that have happened to me in the past and the deaths of my family. It is nice to be able to talk to someone about all of this.

I immersed myself in devotions every morning and started going to a Bible Study for women that has been very enjoyable. It is about the only thing I go out for, the Bible Study and Counseling. Although something good came out of Covid and that is telemedicine. If I do not feel good or am too tired, I can do my counseling online and do not have to wear myself out going to an appointment.

I have always loved Duck Dynasty and we went to see the movie about Phil and Kay Robertson called The Blind. This is one of the things that really encouraged me that no matter what I have done in my past, God will forgive me if I ask him too. I started this book a long time ago, but it took me a long time to write it and get through the trauma I had in my life. I wanted to write so that other people that have been through a lot of trauma understand that there is light at the end of the tunnel. I believe that light is a renewed relationship with Jesus. You do not have to be perfect to be loved by Jesus, in fact the imperfect people are his specialty. He is just waiting for you to decide to welcome him into your life. He is always with you if you look. Even if you are going through horrible things, understand that it is not Jesus doing these things, it is the evil one. He wants to separate us from our Lord and I was not strong enough for a long time to ignore him and look for Jesus. As a mother, I can see that if you introduce your children when they are small, they will come back to Jesus as an adult. I have and now I am living with the fact that I did not do a good job of teaching my children about Jesus. I pray every day for my adult children to turn towards Jesus and accept him into their lives. If this book does nothing else, I want you to be able to see that no matter what you have done in your past Jesus can forgive it all. You only must ask.

JAYDEN

When you left at eighteen, I knew I would see you
again.
You were gone for years serving our country with
honor.
My pride for you was immense, and I worried you
would go to war.
You called me with the news, a disorder that would
send you home.
I wanted to come see you, but you said you would be
okay.
The medication they gave you took the seizures away,
but they came back
With a vengeance and took your life away.
Now all I have is memories of that young boy I knew. I
missed out on the
Years you served and while you grew,

From child to the man that you became, my pride for you was just the same.

I had a year with you, then came a knock on the door. The officer said you died, and so did I that night. My tears will not stop

Flowing. I know that you are safe. With Jesus you spent Christmas as I just sit and wait. For one day I will see you. It can't be soon enough. For Jayden you're my son and my heart is filled with ache.

THE PERFECT STORM

Who knew, except God, that the baby born on a cool, crisp autumn day

Would be taken by the perfect storm.

Who could believe that the chubby-faced toddler, who gave new meaning

To the terrible twos, would succumb to the perfect storm.

Who could see that the boy with the youthful exuberance and smile,

Where the corners of his eyes squinted over and an embarrassed blush, would

Someday see the perfect storm.

Who could look at the strong handsome man that he grew up to be, who

Raised his hand and took an oath to stand and protect our United States,

Would soon be battling the perfect storm.

Then it happened, the perfect storm, where everything aligned perfectly on

A cold November night. No one was ready, least of all his mother, who had

Nurtured, loved unconditionally, and gave life to this child.

The perfect storm is SUDEP or sudden unexplained death in epilepsy. It

Took his life swiftly before anyone knew what was taking place. Everything

Had to be right for the perfect storm to hit.

On Mother's Day, I ponder if anything could have protected my son from

This perfect storm. Can anyone stop this from happening to others? We will

Forever be affected by the perfect storm. It took my son, and it's a battle too

Big for me to take on today. Mother's Day.

www.ingramcontent.com/pod-product-compliance
Lightning Source LLC
Chambersburg PA
CBHW071158130626
46553CB00004B/1702